CHUTZPAH & CHUTZPAH ®

chutzpah (hoo t-spuh)
extreme self-confidence
or audacity.
nerve, cunning, cheek.
the amount of bravery, resolve
or passion a person has.

CHUTZPAH & CHUTZPAH ®

Saatchi & Saatchi: The Insiders' Stories

Richard Myers, Simon Goode and Nick Darke

Michael O'Mara Books Limited

First published in Great Britain in 2017
by Michael O'Mara Books Limited
9 Lion Yard
Tremadoc Road
London SW4 7NQ

ISBN: 978-1-78243-658-4 in paperback print format
ISBN: 978-1-78243-671-3 in ebook format

1 2 3 4 5 6 7 8 9 10

www.mombooks.com

Designed by Nick Darke

Printed and bound by 1010 Printing International Ltd

For Charles and Maurice Saatchi,
whose unique talents and chutzpah
inspired the three of us
and everyone else at Saatchi & Saatchi
to reject mediocrity, to have no fear of being first,
to believe that whatever has gone before
counts for nothing, and that
the unthinkable can be achieved.

AUTHORS' NOTE

We want to thank all contributors to this book. In the few cases where anonymity was requested we have complied.

Given that advertising is a creative business, it's hardly surprising that, over time (and possibly over several drinks), stories may well have evolved and been embellished imaginatively. In short, we'd be foolish to claim that everything in this book is 100 per cent true, and we apologize for any inaccuracies. Our intention was never to harm the reputations of former colleagues or to insult the memory of those who, sadly, are no longer with us.

We want to thank creators and brand owners for allowing their work to be included. Any error or omission in identifying sources is unintentional and every effort has been made to secure clearance and permission.

CONTENTS

FOREWORD

by John Tylee

IT WAS DECEMBER 1994. Maurice Saatchi had been ousted after a shareholder protest at Saatchi & Saatchi. His brother Charles would soon follow him out of the company they'd founded. At the offices of *Campaign* magazine you couldn't move for TV camera crews and microphone-wielding reporters. Unable to find anybody close enough to the action to give them a steer on what had happened – least of all the elusive brothers – the journalists were doing what they invariably do in such situations. They interview each other.

With good connections to both sides of the biggest bust-up in advertising history, *Campaign* was the go-to place for anybody trying to make some sense of it all and speculate on what the outcome might be. As a result Dominic Mills, the editor, and I, as associate editor, found ourselves taking it in turns to give our respective takes.

However, I had a question of my own for a camera crew that had turned up from one particularly far-flung European outpost. What possible interest could this spat be to their viewers? Ah, they replied. This wasn't just any old spat. This was a Saatchi spat. And everybody had heard of the Saatchis.

True, of course. But why? How had Maurice and Charles accumulated so much charisma – and chutzpah – that the public's fascination with them extended well beyond the UK? It wasn't that they loved the limelight. Indeed, they made every attempt to avoid it. Small wonder that you admired their audacity as much as you cursed their cussedness.

This, however, seemed only to make them even more intriguing. I met Charles just once. It was in 1998 at an M&C Saatchi Christmas drinks party for *Campaign*. He was nothing like I expected. On the contrary, he seemed so consumed by shyness that his eyes were fixed on his shoes. I don't remember much about our brief conversation. Only being surprised and flattered to hear from a man said to be so demanding of his staff that he often read what I wrote and enjoyed it.

Maurice, in contrast, was the most seductive charmer I've met. His interviews – rare and invariably off the record – were always conducted sotto voce. By leaning close to hear what he was saying, you felt he was sharing information with you that he'd never divulged to anybody else. At the end, he'd walk you to the agency's front door and shake hands. You wondered how any new business prospect could possibly resist.

Inevitably, the brothers' legacy is a mixed one. Their group was an astonishing breeding ground for talent. How many agencies can boast of providing four members of the Upper House – Maurice himself along with Tim Bell, John Sharkey and Michael Dobbs? Five if you count a one-time Saatchi trainee called Karren Brady. And what other agency could claim to have so influenced Britain's social and political course with 'Labour Isn't Working', the poster that helped propel Margaret Thatcher to power in 1979?

Yet in trying to change the ad industry so quickly and comprehensively, hubris sometimes ran ahead of common sense. There's little doubt that the mind-boggling $450 million the Saatchi group paid for advertising firm Ted Bates in 1986 caused clients to question whether they should be coughing up 15 per cent commission when big agencies seemed awash with cash. Nevertheless, perhaps history will take a more charitable view of times when it seemed the brothers had taken leave of their senses. While the 1987 proposal to acquire the Midland Bank might have seemed insane, you could argue that, in the light of subsequent events, it could have forced the banking industry to become more customer-centric and less reckless.

What's certain is that the brothers were never scared of trying something to see what would happen. In doing so they helped ensure British advertising could do anything the Americans could do – and often do it better. No wonder that they still attract controversy and fascination in equal measure.

John Tylee is a former associate editor of Campaign *and continues to write regularly for the magazine.*

INTRODUCTION

THE IDEA FOR THIS BOOK was conceived on a long drive through France by Simon Goode and a fellow ex-Saatchi colleague. With nearly sixty years at Saatchi & Saatchi between them, they started recalling stories of their days at the agency as they left Calais in the north-east and didn't stop until they reached Cognac in the south-west. And then carried on throughout the return journey. Simon realized he wasn't alone in having interesting stories to tell about his days at the agency, and that he wasn't the only Saatchi & Saatchi person with a unique insight into this fascinating company.

It also occurred to Simon that although the astonishing rise of Saatchi & Saatchi, from small London agency founded in 1970 by Charles and his younger brother Maurice Saatchi, to global advertising giant less than two decades later had been well documented, they could tell a very different story. It would be the first book about Saatchis made up of stories told by people who had been there at the time, who knew first-hand what it was really like working with the Saatchi brothers and witnessing the fairly spectacular evolution of a very special corporate entity.

So Simon started to ask around, beginning with Saatchi people he knew who had contributed to the company's extraordinary success. These people in turn contacted colleagues they knew for their stories. It was immediately clear that the vast majority were not just willing to contribute but were really enthusiastic about the project, too. The search and harvest took about two years.

Meanwhile, Simon recruited friend and fellow Saatchi lifer Richard Myers to write the book. During his near thirty years at Saatchis and as general manager of the Europe, Middle East and Africa network, Simon had a unique insight into what made this extraordinary company tick. But copywriter Richard Myers would be the one to pull all the stories together – he had decades of writing experience under his belt, having helped create advertising for many of Saatchis top clients. He also has a significant knowledge of the company, having been joint creative director of the London agency, chairman of the company's first European Creative Board, a member of the Worldwide Creative Board and executive creative director responsible for Saatchis' own brand. Completing the trio is designer Nick Darke, one of Saatchi & Saatchi's earliest recruits. After being creative director of the Saatchi & Saatchi-owned design company Siegel & Gale in the late 1980s, Nick became creative director of Saatchi & Saatchi Design.

We three have always felt privileged to have been part of a truly remarkable company, densely populated by daring and ingenious talents, and by big and eccentric personalities. And judging by the reactions of those approached for their stories, we are not alone in feeling this way. In total, well over 200 people responded with stories which provided the ingredients for a very rich corporate cocktail of irreverence, brilliance, talent, tantrums, laughs, stunts, pratfalls, naughtiness, fearlessness, humanity, outrageousness, eccentricity, daring, excess, wows and oops.

Our book's title springs from the company's motto – nothing is impossible – and the fact that chutzpah was the essential fuel that drove the company forward and helped it achieve the apparently impossible.

This first-hand account of the highs and lows of an iconic advertising company with a unique corporate DNA showcases the extraordinary actions and attitudes that created and probably still sustains an inimitable business. This book could be read as an entertaining business book, or perhaps seen as a timeless guide to what it takes to take a business sector apart by being brave, mildly indifferent to rules and wholly indifferent to what has gone before.

However, what *Chutzpah & Chutzpah* could not be mistaken for is a novel. The plot would be beyond belief. Imagine the synopsis: two brothers start a London advertising agency. Ambition: to be the world's biggest agency. One brother is highly creative and reclusive. The other, a very smart businessman. Three years on, the agency moves into a prestigious building to create the illusion that they've made it big time. A year after that, through acquisition they double in size. Within a decade of starting up, the agency is the UK's biggest, and they help the UK's first female prime minister get elected. The agency sets out to buy a high-street bank. Within two decades of starting, ambition is achieved: the agency does become the world's biggest. Ultimately, perhaps the best description of *Chutzpah & Chutzpah* is that it is a story of applied creativity.

Richard Myers, Simon Goode and Nick Darke
London 2016

Chapter 1

NAME THE FIRST ADVERTISING AGENCY THAT COMES INTO YOUR HEAD.

EXACTLY

Advertising agencies make their money by making their clients famous, and yet advertising agencies are anonymous out in the real world. With one exception.

IN 1989, THE OUTDOOR ADVERTISING COMPANY, Maiden, launched a competition inviting agencies to submit ideas to promote themselves on a big Spectacolor screen in Piccadilly Circus, London's neon light centre. Saatchi & Saatchi's entry, created by copywriter Adam Keen and art director Antony Easton, came in two parts. The first half of the message read 'NAME THE FIRST ADVERTISING AGENCY THAT COMES INTO YOUR HEAD', which was followed, after a brief blank screen, with 'EXACTLY'.

But how did Saatchi & Saatchi's unique fame come about? It was almost certainly driven at least by the recognition that fame is priceless and in turn fame begets fortunes. Of course, it's one thing to recognize the value of something like fame, but it's quite another to make sure you get more than your fair share of it.

How, for a start, do you make your company interesting enough for it to be constantly written and talked about? How do you step out from the shadows cast by your clients? The good news is you don't necessarily have to turn yourself into a media tart, attending as many high-profile events as possible and providing gossip columns with their lifeblood. In fact, in Saatchi & Saatchi's case, the very opposite – being reclusive – paid huge fame dividends.

For Charles Saatchi, being reclusive meant not appearing in public unless it was absolutely necessary. He may not be Howard Hughes but he has gone to great, and occasionally bizarre lengths to avoid meeting people – clients in particular. Many people tell the following story, but Ron Leagas, who would later become managing director of Saatchi & Saatchi before leaving to start up his own agency, saw the action first-hand. It revolves around a significant new business pitch for Singer Sewing Machines:

'I recall starting the pitch around lunchtime in the basement meeting room [of Saatchi & Saatchi's original Golden Square offices] and, true to form, found myself distracted from my earnest pitch by the sight of Charlie watching the meeting from the adjacent room through the tiny film projector window. The pitch was going well

but it went on and on with Brian Goshawk [marketing director] and Gill Lewis [marketing manager] quizzing and probing us mercilessly. We finally ascended the spiral staircase to see them off at around 7 p.m. By this time, Charlie had deserted his spy post and found himself exposed on the ground floor as the only person there. Fearing he would have to be introduced to this important prospect, he pretended to be a cleaner, screwing up an ad layout and using it as a cleaning cloth.'

It's a moot point whether Charles's reclusiveness sprang from his shyness or from his strategic nous, because Charles was certainly no shrinking violet when it came to dealing with the press. He was an expert at publicity management and his sense of how to control information was acute.

John Tylee, a former associate editor of the advertising industry magazine *Campaign*, recalls Charles's way of working with the media (or should that be working the media?): 'Having close links with the trade press was, of course, essential and the agency was adept at cultivating those links. Nobody was better at it than Charles, who kept *Campaign* supplied with a constant stream of news tips. So many, in fact, that when he announced the formation of Saatchi & Saatchi in September 1970, the magazine splashed with the story. In the light of subsequent events, it was the right decision. But at the time, the news probably merited no more than a modest spot on page three. The reason it got bumped up was because *Campaign* felt indebted to one of its best sources.'

By all accounts, Charles was little short of hyperactive when it came to publicity. According to Saatchi & Saatchi's first ever account executive, John Honsinger, the amount of publicity that Saatchis got throughout its early years was 'largely down to Charlie or inspired by him, which demonstrates his sheer inventiveness. He would regularly phone *Campaign* to place stories and rumours. The effect of which was to get the industry talking and, in turn, *Campaign* would tip him off when an account was about to move. A story might be that a company was unhappy with its agency, which would cause them to issue a denial and sometimes result in a review of the business.'

Ron Leagas remembers Charles's calls to *Campaign*, 'Garnering favour by telling of rumours he'd picked up. In reality, the rumours initially were recycled stories he'd plucked from the columns of *The Grocer* magazine.' At least two people recall Charles using a different name when 'placing' stories; holding his nose to create a nasal-sounding anonymity, he became Jack Robinson.

Sean O'Connor joined Saatchi & Saatchi as an account handler in summer 1974: 'Charles had one overriding objective for the agency in those days and that was to make it famous. His ambition each week was to be the lead story on the cover of *Campaign*. A friend of mine had once added up all the new business wins they (Saatchis) had announced in their first two years and it came to over £30 million. This was in the days when that would be the total billings for a decent top-five agency. They'd announce anything. Their great friends, the Green brothers, once had the idea of selling on the dresses that catwalk models wore. They opened a small shop in London's Bond Street and gave the "account" to the Saatchis. The story duly ran on *Campaign*'s front page as "Saatchis in £3m retail win". This was when the agency's entire billings were about that number.'

An early employee of Saatchi & Saatchi was the then art director (later Sir) John Hegarty, co-founder of Bartle Bogle Hegarty. In his book, *Hegarty on Advertising,* he recalls some publicity creation from his time at Saatchi & Saatchi:

'Charles could invent stories out of nothing as well: there was an occasion when there wasn't much to report, no news stories to keep the agency at the front of the trade media's mind…On this particular occasion Charles wanted to create a story that underlined the value of his creative department, so he contacted a friend in the insurance business and agreed with this associate that he'd "insure" the Saatchi & Saatchi creative department for £1,000,000, a vast sum of money in the early seventies. On top of that, Charles decided he'd take a leaf out of the world of football and institute a transfer fee if any other agency wanted to poach one of his highly valuable creatives. The story was complete fiction. But a few days later there we all were, the creative department of Saatchi & Saatchi, on the back page of *The Sunday Times* business section, photographed on a bench in Golden Square posing like a football team.'

It was (designer of this book) Nick Darke's very first week at Saatchis when the photograph was taken. For some reason (and it's still a mystery to Darke) Charles told him he'd decided to give him the name 'Philip James' in the caption to the photograph.

Nick Crean became Charles and Maurice's PA in the late 1970s. He was no stranger to the importance Charles placed on managing stories about Saatchis in the media. According to Nick, one of Maurice and Charles's legendary exchanges of views – complete with office trashing – was caused by a front cover of *Marketing Week*, headed 'A Tale of Two Saatchis'. The story in the magazine was critical of the two brothers. Charles blamed Maurice for talking to a journalist without asking him. Nick says, 'Not only had I been summoned into the office at dawn to make sure that all copies of that week's *Marketing Week* were removed from everyone's desk and from reception, I was dispatched to buy up all the copies from all the newsagents in the Charlotte Street area.'

John Tylee joined *Campaign* in the mid-1980s and was amazed at how far the Saatchis would take story management: 'The swashbuckling way in which Saatchi & Saatchi went about building its reputation was in sharp contrast to the control freakery that kicked in when it came to maintaining its desired image. While most agencies allowed you free access to almost anybody you wished to talk to, Saatchis had pulled the wagons into a circle. Only a small group of senior executives – and nobody else – were allowed to be quoted. The result was often utter farce. I once phoned a bright young Charlotte Street manager called Paul Bainsfair with the news that he was to be a *Campaign* "Face to Watch" and could he help me with a few career details. Sorry, he replied, he wasn't allowed to. Only the top brass could do that.'

However, media management wasn't the only weapon in Saatchi & Saatchi's armoury. The fame of the agency had something of a head start. The surname the brothers were born with was a brilliant brand name. It was unusual but it wasn't difficult to remember. One could even view it as an object lesson when it comes to naming a product, a service or a company. In short, be different, be brave. Using the name twice also hinted at a highly respectable profession, such as a company of lawyers or accountants, thus making it more client-friendly. The brothers shrewdly avoided a made-up name that might have had temporary appeal before it would quickly begin to seem dated.

SAATCHI & SAATCHI

The 'establishment' feel of the chosen name was enhanced by basing the logo on the clever choice of a classic, conservative, but elegant typeface, Goudy Old Style. The logo appeared in a number of random variations until Nick Darke formalized it and set the rules for the logo's usage.

Ultimately, though, no one would dispute the greatest catalyst of Saatchi & Saatchi's unparalleled household fame was winning the Conservative Party account in 1978. The style of political advertising created by Saatchi & Saatchi for the Conservative Party had never been seen before in the UK. Until then, political advertising amounted to polite or pompous, but always meaningless slogans. It was the birth of a new brand of political advertising that attacked other parties. It was aggressive, but it was also thought-provoking.

LABOUR ISN'T WORKING.

UNEMPLOYMENT OFFICE

BRITAIN'S BETTER OFF WITH THE CONSERVATIVES.

The Labour politician Denis Healey denounced the poster in parliament, saying the Conservatives had reached a new low by selling politics like soap powder.

Leading the charge was a poster, written by Andrew Rutherford and art directed by Martyn Walsh, showing a long queue of people outside an employment office. The headline, aimed directly at the governing political party, simply stated: 'LABOUR ISN'T WORKING'.

It caused a sensation. Naturally, accusations of dirty tricks flew around. For instance, it was claimed that the people in the queue were agency employees, which was denied. Importantly, the creators of this controversial work didn't remain anonymously in the shadows. Saatchi & Saatchi shared the spotlight with their client. The agency began to be mentioned by name on television and in all the press, broadsheet and tabloid alike. This was too high profile an opportunity to be missed and the moment was seized with all available hands. The advertising was provocative and for once, here was some political advertising that was meaningful. The company was becoming a household name, picked up by journalists, commentators, comedians and the general public. And spat out by all those who opposed Conservative Party values. The first campaign for the Conservatives led to victory in the 1979 general election, and the appointment of Britain's first female prime minister, Margaret Thatcher. Britain would never be the same again.

Without doubt, Saatchi & Saatchi's fortunes were changed and secured by their association with the top level of the British establishment. But at the heart of its success was the agency's creative work and being responsible for some of the most talked-about and memorable advertising of the last fifty years. For example, the line, 'AUSTRALIANS WOULDN'T GIVE A XXXX FOR

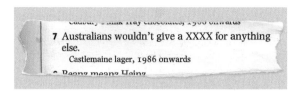

7 Australians wouldn't give a XXXX for anything else.
Castlemaine lager, 1986 onwards

~~Beanz meanz Heinz~~

ANYTHING ELSE', written by James Lowther for Castlemaine XXXX lager, can be found in the *Oxford Dictionary of Quotations* and the word Strimmer, which Richard Myers invented for Black & Decker, is now the generic name for this type of gardening tool. There are also lines from hugely successful brand advertising such as 'THE WORLD'S FAVOURITE AIRLINE', for British Airways, 'IT IS. ARE YOU?' to launch the *Independent* newspaper, 'WHY SLOWMO WHEN YOU CAN FLYMO?' and 'WHY NOT?' for Lanson champagne – Saatchis had the edge on ingenious campaign lines as well as a shrewd eye for publicity.

'WORLD PROBLEMS. WORLD SOLUTIONS. WORLD CLASS.' was written for ICI, but it could easily apply to Saatchi & Saatchi and its work. The company's unique fame was highly magnetic and, as such, attracted new business and top creative and management talent. For any employee of the company at the time, being asked at a social event who they worked for was the cue for a pleasing glow of recognition to wash over them when they replied 'Saatchis'.

Similarly, the agency's clients got a buzz from telling friends and relative strangers that their agency was Saatchis. In fact, on occasion, there was the suspicion that some clients only awarded their accounts to Saatchis so they could boast about who their agency was. This often became clear when they found the agency's creative ideas just a little too creative for their taste, and wanted something more ordinary. Many members of the agency's creative department experienced the ensuing culture clash that could be messy and deeply unsatisfying for all concerned.

The fame magnet attracted its fair share of unusual new business prospects. Media group director Stephen Traveller recalls taking the train north to Retford in Nottinghamshire with account director Paul Hammersley to meet a prospective client who had approached the agency saying, 'I'm well aware of what you've done for Maggie and I want some of your famous Saatchi & Saatchi magic dust sprinkled on my business'.

The prospective client was a funeral director and unsurprisingly, he picked up Traveller and Hammersley at Retford Station in a vintage hearse. They had a grand, in-depth tour of the funeral parlour, followed by an invitation to lunch. Back in the hearse they found themselves being taken to Lincoln, the best part of thirty miles from Retford. After lunch, any hopes of an immediate lift back to Retford for their train home were dashed. The would-be client insisted on a tour of Lincoln Cathedral.

After a considerable period of time, the party was joined by the cathedral choirmaster. The agency pair were a little mystified by this turn of events and by the choirmaster's stated ambition to turn the choir into an international success. The undertaker offered a simple explanation. 'Well, this gentleman is a very old friend of mine and when I mentioned you were coming to see me today, I suggested you might be able to sprinkle some of your famous Saatchi & Saatchi magic dust over his choir as well!' Although an advertising campaign was created for the funeral parlour, it never saw the light of day. As Traveller ruefully observed, 'I don't think they realized that money was involved in our making a living.'

A negative flip side of fame is remembered by typographer Dave Wood, who recalls being told exactly where to go by an anti-Thatcher London cabbie, when he'd asked to be taken to Saatchi's

offices in Charlotte Street. And Robin Murtough, a Saatchi copywriter, recalls how an art director from the agency was caught using a forged annual railway season ticket. The story generated glaring headlines in the national press, such as 'Saatchi Art Chief in Forgery Scandal'. If he'd worked anywhere else, Murtough observes, the story would probably not have even been reported. Around the same time, long-serving Saatchi & Saatchi receptionist Gill Chapman (formerly Collett) remembers the agency being targeted by an anti-capitalist demonstration called 'Stop the City'. The demonstrators invaded the agency, trashed reception and set off smoke bombs. Ah, the price of fame.

And the price of fame took many forms as the celebrity of the agency and of its founders grew to national proportions. On one occasion the price of fame was exactly £3,000 when account handler Tom Holmes recklessly, but successfully, bid that amount for the puppet heads of the 'Snaatchi & Snaatchi brothers' from the satirical TV programme *Spitting Image*, in a charity event auction.

Holmes's considerable hangover the next day was made even worse by the sight of the two rubber heads in his bedroom, and the horrible realization that he'd blown a quarter of his annual salary on them. His immediate boss was profoundly unsympathetic and told him to take the puppets to Charles and Maurice and explain himself to them. Holmes was delighted (and relieved) to discover Charles and Maurice weren't there, so he left a note with the heads.

A nervous few hours followed. Returning to his desk, Holmes discovered a message from Maurice, thanking him for his initiative 'in saving the heads from falling into another agency's hands'. The £3,000 bill was paid. No one else from advertising was ever featured on *Spitting Image* for the simple reason that no one else from advertising was ever as universally famous or notorious as Charles and Maurice Saatchi.

There is no doubt how pivotal winning the Conservative Party account was to Saatchi & Saatchi's unique household fame. Maurice Saatchi later acknowledged its significance at an event held in 2010 at the Saatchi Gallery (where else?), celebrating the company's fortieth birthday. In fact, the birthday party brought together both Saatchi & Saatchi and M&C Saatchi for the first time, in public, since the acrimonious split in

Lady Thatcher and Sir John Major at the 'Saatchistory' fortieth anniversary party.

1995 (see page 15). It was attended by two former British prime ministers (Thatcher and Major), many other high-ranking politicians, and other luminaries such as Lord (Andrew) Lloyd-Webber, Alastair Campbell, Lord (Peter) Mandelson, playwright Sir David Hare and his wife, fashion designer Nicole Farhi, Sir Nicholas Soames and Lord (Stuart) Rose of Marks & Spencer fame. Charles Saatchi maintained his usual approach to parties and did not attend.

Chapter 2

THE REALITY OF ILLUSION

Businesses can learn a lot from magicians.
And from their earliest days, Saatchi & Saatchi
understood and exploited the power of illusion
to create a desired reality in the minds of clients
and potential clients, suppliers, potential
high-talent employees and the media.

WHAT'S THE REALITY you want people to believe about you? Do you want to appear as small as you actually are, or larger? As successful as you are or more successful? Do you want to look like a bit player or a big player? An enduring illusion about Saatchi & Saatchi was that it only produced highly creative award-winning advertising. Not so. There were always clients on the roster who wanted only run-of-the-mill campaigns. But they were still profitable pieces of business.

The essence of the illusion business is, forget 'what you see is what you get' and go for 'what you see is what you think you get'.

John Honsinger (see Chapter 1), the first account executive hired by Saatchi & Saatchi, recalls working in the Golden Square offices the company occupied when first set up in 1970: 'In those early days there were only twenty to thirty staff, but Charles Saatchi wanted the place to look busier than that small number of people could naturally suggest. So regularly, when there was an important client coming in for a meeting, everyone was instructed to rush around purposefully and make a lot of noise. Sometimes, when even that fell short of the desired illusion, people would be pulled in off the street and paid to sit or stand around in the reception area.'

A similar strategy was employed later as Saatchi & Saatchi was establishing itself in Saudi Arabia. A significant break for the fledgling company came when they were included on Saudi American Bank's pitch list for the launch of the first credit card in Saudi Arabia. Certain key positions, however, had still not been filled at the new office. Creative director Ed Jones managed to hire an art director, and Mike Liebling was brought in from the London office for some clever strategic thinking. There was, however, a very significant link still missing: an Arabic-speaking copywriter. A very rare species. Gerry Nagle, the managing director, explains how he overcame the problem:

'I was out shopping in Jeddah and having a coffee when I saw a chap who seemed down on his luck, selling his books of poetry. This was Nizar, and his English was very good. I figured he could translate the copy created by an English copywriter, so why not give it a go?'

Nagle's gamble paid off and Nizar later became a key player.

The next issue Nagle faced was the fact that the Jeddah office had just five employees in total, and when the client visited he would be underwhelmed by this sparse team. Nagle solved the problem:

'At prayer time, I grabbed a load of chaps from the mosque and spread them around the office. The client was mightily impressed by the number of locals we had on our staff, and it helped us win the pitch.'

The illusion was played out in Korea too. US-born account director Peter Levitan says he

'had to run the staff of our Seoul office up and down the stairs to be in different places, so the Northwest (Airlines) client prospect thought we were a larger agency'.

There's an enhanced version of the people illusion – the whole agency illusion. In 1995, after Charles and Maurice had been driven out of the company they had founded by a shareholder revolt in the previous December, they and the senior management who left with them were not allowed to work – they were on gardening leave. Mike Russell-Hills, a film producer and director who had been deeply involved in the creation of many of Saatchi & Saatchi's famous party political broadcasts for the Conservative Party, was hired to film the breakaway group actually gardening at (now ex-chairman, Saatchi & Saatchi plc) Jeremy Sinclair's house. There was a more serious motive behind this though. The purpose was to show British Airways, whose account they wanted to follow them from the original agency,

A fierce legal battle failed to secure 'Saatchi & Saatchi' for the brothers to use as their company name.

that they were active and ready for business as M&C Saatchi.

It worked. They were asked to present to Lord King, the airline's president. There was a slight snag. They didn't have an office. So they rented one for not much longer than the presentation was expected to last. The office was dressed to look like the real thing, with the M&C Saatchi logo stuck to the front door with double-sided tape. Within ten minutes of the presentation ending and the clients leaving the building, the furniture was already on its way back to the prop-hire company. Just as everyone was preparing to leave the now empty office space, there was a call to say that British Airways' chairman and CEO Colin (later Lord) Marshall had forgotten his briefcase and was on the way back to collect it. With a group of secretaries, Maurice Saatchi waited outside the office building clutching the briefcase, so no one from British Airways would re-enter the building. The illusion remained intact.

More permanent property, cleverly chosen and cunningly negotiated for, can play a major role in sending illusionary signals to the outside world.

Saatchi & Saatchi's first significant property illusion came from its move, in 1974, from its offices in Golden Square which it had outgrown, to 15 Lower Regent Street nearby. It was the shipping line Cunard's former property. It had a vast twenty-metre showroom window frontage and a very impressive reception area, visible from the street through an expanse of glass. To the creative department, most of whom had to work with no natural light in the cramped bowels of the building, this soon became known as the 'deception area'. Paul Bainsfair, who would later

The former Cunard building at 15 Lower Regent Street.

become joint managing director, candidly describes the property as 'wholly inappropriate office space. No rooms to work in. No space, but it had a huge reception.' Strategic planner David Keig summarizes it as, '75 per cent reception area – to impress – and just 25 per cent office space'.

Account handler Sean O'Connor reckons the property had what the agency stood for – plenty of front. Somewhat more poetically he talks of how

'a vast glass window showed passing pedestrians our colossal reception area. And inside there was an ocean liner's observation rail that one could lean on to look out into the rolling waves of traffic.'

O'Connor also reports that years later Tim Bell (who had then been managing director) told him that the rent on the place was three times the agency's income at the time. The price of giving the impression that the agency had truly arrived was quite high. Fortunately, business growth, probably aided by the illusion, was sufficiently spectacular to cover that particular bill.

The Saatchi & Saatchi 'corporate cathedral' at the bottom of Berkeley Square.

A second property illusion was engineered at the dawn of the 1990s. Berkeley Square had been the London home of rival agency J. Walter Thompson for ever. So it must have been disturbing for them to discover, one morning, that the new building across the square had the name 'Saatchi & Saatchi' emblazoned across its front, looking like a genuine corporate cathedral. And looking like a threat, too. It appeared to JWT that the whole of Saatchi & Saatchi must be moving in on their territory. But again, the illusion and the facts were some distance apart. In reality, only Charles and Maurice Saatchi, and Jeremy Sinclair, plus their support staff, had moved in, taking up just a tiny fraction of the overall space in the building. Yes, Saatchis had taken the head lease, but they'd sublet four floors (for instance, to GlaxoSmithKline). Yet, cannily, they'd negotiated the right to have their name up there on the building. According to Simon Mellor, director, Saatchi & Saatchi Plc, and later commercial director, Saatchi & Saatchi EMEA (Europe, Middle East and Africa),

'GSK were mighty pissed off that we gazumped them to this right.'

Not so much a corporate cathedral, more a corporate fascia. If there were a Nobel Prize for illusion creation, Charles Saatchi would have won it any number of times. He has always been the complete master of the art. In his book, *Hegarty on Advertising*, former Saatchi art director John Hegarty recalls how astute Charles was right from the start, and how critical illusions can be to a company's success:

'Our ambition was that the agency's reputation was to be one of unsurpassed creativity. Charles, realizing this could also frighten clients, had his hair cut short, bought shirts from Turnbull & Asser and started to wear conservative suits and club ties. Using the same "don't frighten the clients" logic, the agency's letterhead was designed to make us look like a bank rather than a creative hot shop. It was about reassurance and, of course, maintaining the illusion.'

Charles Saatchi was responsible for some illusion of his own. When a Saatchi client felt so unloved because he had never had any contact with a Saatchi brother that he was threatening to take his business away, Charles employed a little theatre. Bill Muirhead, who was responsible for the unloved client and unable to contact Maurice, who was on a yacht in the Caribbean, tried desperately to get Charles to talk to him. But Charles didn't talk to clients. In the end, Muirhead said, 'Then say goodbye to £8 million.'

Charles replied, 'Wait a minute, you say he's never talked to a Saatchi brother?'

'No,' said Muirhead, 'that's the problem.'

'OK then, I'll ring him up and say I'm Maurice.' The client was none the wiser and decided to stick with the Saatchis.

This wasn't the only example of Saatchis being masters of

illusion on a smaller, personal scale. A client wanted a more mature account person on their business, but group account director Paul Cowan wanted the youthful Paul Houlding to do the job. So Houlding was dispatched to the opticians where he purchased a pair of spectacles with plain glass, thus creating the requested older man.

Charles Saatchi was as reluctant to mingle with Saatchi & Saatchi employees socially as he was to meet clients, but as his one-time PA Simon Mellor recalls, there was still an illusion job to be done:

'Every year, when there was a big Christmas party, Charles would refuse to go. But everyone in the company wanted him to be there. He would tell me he would not go but that I should pretend I had seen him. So I would be at the party and people would ask me if Charles was there. "Yes," I would say, pointing to the other side of the room, "I just saw him over there." Asked again, I would point the other way, or say I'd seen him having a drink, or on his way to the loo. Eventually it would get late enough for me to say that Charles had gone home. Which had been true since before the party started.'

Ultimately, Charles's reluctance to meet clients and his commitment to maintaining a low personal profile did an excellent job of enhancing the mystique surrounding him. But any thought that Charles's mastery of illusion only applied to his business life would be quite wrong.

It seems as if chutzpah and an ability to create illusions have always been in Charles's makeup, equally evident in his private life as well as in business. The often-told story of Charles's run-in while driving his newly acquired Rolls-Royce is a case in point. Charles was driving it through Soho when he had to stop behind a van that was blocking the road. Charles impatiently put his hand on the horn and kept it there. Before long, the van driver got out to confront

Charles. Calmly, Charles lowered his window a little. He looked the van driver right in the eye with due menace, and gestured that he had his hand inside his jacket. Together with a few well-chosen words, the illusionary gun was sufficient to resolve the stand-off and to get the van moved. In another version of the story, Charles had a passenger in the car, the commercials director Sid Roberson. Sid was a bodybuilder and had a mean look about him. In reality, Sid didn't like trouble, but he looked very convincing as a bodyguard. When Charles gestured towards him with, again, due menace and a few choice words, the illusion was powerful and threatening enough to convince the other driver to retreat.

As magicians know, fooling all of the people all of the time takes more than chutzpah alone. It requires meticulous planning, backed up by an ability to think imaginatively on one's feet at lightning speed, should the meticulous planning turn out to be anything but. Apparently, Maurice Saatchi boarded a train to the north of England with a thick file of notes on the prospective client he was going to meet. When he opened the file he discovered it contained nothing but blank paper. In the meeting he slammed the file down on the table with a dash of theatre and said, 'Look, I've read all of this. We all know all of this.

Now, what's your real problem?'

It may sound perverse, but in the early 1980s Saatchi & Saatchi pitched for an account simply to create an illusion. The company was invited by existing client British Leyland to pitch for more of their business, the relaunch of the Rover SD1. Bill Muirhead ran the Leyland account, but for this pitch Charles chose account director David Miller to run it because the new Leyland management team were looking for a brand-building FMCG (fast-moving consumer goods) man. Miller was briefed by a 'clearly hostile' ad manager, Lawson Pater, and reported back to Charles that things didn't look too promising. Charles didn't seem at all phased by this news. Just do a great job, he said, money no object.

Three weeks and £35,000 later, an extraordinary campaign was pitched. It broke every rule in the car advertising handbook, using sophisticated New Yorker-style cartoons instead of photography.

"...and another reason I bought this new Rover if you must know Dankworth, is its new larger rear window... because one doesn't get to the top in the hack-biting hurly burly of the cocoa-bean commodity market without making damn sure you can see who's coming up behind you."

THE NEW '82 ROVERS ▓ DRIVING AMBITIONS FULFILLED.

Losing this new business pitch mattered far less than not taking part.

Created by the group (which included Richard Myers) led by James Lowther and Martyn Walsh, it was utterly Rover, but would be way over the heads of the Leyland management. Tim Bell's view of the campaign was that it was brilliant, it wouldn't win Saatchis the business, but to go ahead with it anyway. All of those involved in the campaign's creation were naturally very proud of this analysis. Miller challenged Charles on this 'exercise in apparent futility'. 'Didn't you notice?' Charles asked, 'While you were pitching, we were buying [the advertising agency] Dorlands? We didn't want anything to depress our share price, and pulling out of a Leyland pitch would have done just that.'

But perhaps the grandest illusion in the story of Saatchi & Saatchi is the reverse takeover of Garland-Compton. Back in 1973, the Saatchi brothers had a simple declared ambition: to be the biggest advertising agency in the world. They were realistic enough to realize that acquisition would be the only way to achieve their ambition.

A number of polite (but no doubt surprising) approach letters to rival agencies proposing their takeover by Saatchi & Saatchi yielded nothing (other than a reported response from Jack Wynne-Williams of Masius Wynne-Williams saying he'd checked in petty cash to see if there was enough to buy Saatchi & Saatchi). One of the agencies not to receive a letter from the brothers was Garland-Compton. This, apparently, offended its chairman Kenneth Gill.

Around the same time, Gill was looking for a way to expand and invigorate his agency. In the end, what led to the reverse takeover was a coincidence. Maurice Saatchi, unaware of Gill's ambition, called Garland-Compton's managing director Ron Rimmer to ask if he would become Saatchi & Saatchi's business manager. Rimmer told Gill about the call. Gill encouraged him to meet Maurice and find out all he could. Rimmer's report of his meeting with Maurice led Gill to see that Saatchi & Saatchi could be the ideal match for his objectives. Gill approached Charles and Maurice and months of negotiations followed.

The appeal of Garland-Compton grew on the Saatchis. They could see three significant benefits. Instant growth was one. Major clients such as Rowntrees and Procter & Gamble was a second. And the third was getting a toehold in the US through Compton New York, a 49 per cent shareholder in Garland-Compton.

Gill sought the advice of his friend, businessman James Gulliver, who owned around 10 per cent of Compton shares. Because he was busy with a series of other investments he was making at the time, he got one of his smart young employees to help with Gill's request. His name was (the future Sir) Martin Sorrell. When Gulliver briefed him about the proposed takeover of Saatchi & Saatchi, Sorrell knew the name but didn't know it was an advertising agency (these were the days before the famous 1979 Conservative campaign). He'd seen the name on their Lower Regent Street offices. Apparently, he said he thought it was a new Japanese hi-fi firm. (From this rather inauspicious start something of a mutual admiration society developed between the Saatchi brothers and Sorrell, who later became the financial director of their much-enlarged company.)

A deal was finally struck. The Saatchis would sell their business to Compton for shares. They would own a 36 per cent share. Compton of New York's holding would be diluted down from 49 per cent to 26 per cent. The balance of the shares were held by public shareholders. Each side had a non-negotiable point. The brothers insisted the Saatchi & Saatchi name had to be retained. This, of course, was critical to the illusion that Saatchis were taking over. Initial resistance from Gill and his associates folded, and the name Saatchi & Saatchi Garland-Compton was adopted.

Gill's non-negotiable point was that the whole of Saatchi & Saatchi had to move into Garland-Compton's offices in Charlotte Street. In comparable circumstances, this move could have undermined the illusion of who was taking over whom, but not in this case. Remarkably, the negotiations and then the deal were kept secret, but just a week before the deal was due to be announced, the now defunct trade paper, *Ad Weekly*, carried a rare interview with Charles Saatchi. Charles was asked which agencies' creative work

he admired. Richard Myers recalls reading Charles's response. All the usual suspects were listed – CDP, BMP and so on – but Charles also cited Garland-Compton, which was incongruous and strange. To Kenneth Gill, however, it wasn't so unexplained, and he phoned Charles, angrily saying he'd blown it. But only Bob Gross, the chairman of Geers Gross put two and two together. He called Gill, said 'Congratulations' and rang off.

Gill wanted the announcement to make it clear that the deal was a merger, not an acquisition. One can only imagine how shocking it must have been for Gill to read the headline splashed across the front page of the other trade paper, *Campaign*:

'SAATCHI SWALLOWS UP THE COMPTON GROUP'.

Although the story beneath the headline was factually accurate, the headline was enough to create the ultimate and irreversible illusion, which, of course, before very long became the reality.

But perhaps the role of illusion was most neatly encapsulated by Maurice Saatchi in one simple exchange with Didier Colmet-Daâge, one time managing director of Saatchi & Saatchi France. Colmet-Daâge was asking Maurice what he thought made the company so successful, suggesting, for example, 'the accumulation of young and bright people, totally committed and ready to work night and day, for a portion of a salary because it was for Saatchi...' Maurice cut him off sharply at this point. 'No Didier, there's only one thing critical to all this: hype.'

Ultimately there's a vast difference between the magician's illusion and the business illusion. The magician's is just a temporary illusion. The business illusion has a bigger ultimate objective – to create a new reality.

Chapter 3

A HIGHER WAY TO HIRE

Needless to say, Saatchi & Saatchi's style of recruitment doesn't follow a strict process. Or any process, frankly. After all, if you use rigid, conventional hiring processes it could follow that you end up hiring only unremarkable people.

A VERY COMMON APPROACH to recruitment for white-collar businesses is the Oxbridge graduate route. But is this really the only source of the right stuff? This unimaginative approach to hiring is coming increasingly into question, but Saatchis were ahead of the game in the seventies and eighties. In fact, people have ended up working at Saatchi & Saatchi for, some would say, quite bizarre reasons. But the company's success depends on it being populated by extraordinary people particularly, but certainly not exclusively, in the creative department. The thing is, extraordinary people often defy convention and the usual rules of interview responses and neat CVs.

One of the earliest recruits was Jeremy Sinclair, the company's first creative director. He actually joined Cramer Saatchi, the creative consultancy set up by Ross Cramer and Charles Saatchi that predated the agency. Sinclair, typically, didn't see it as a buyer's market when he first met Charles Saatchi for a job. 'He'll do,' is how he describes his encounter with Charles. In other words, it was he who chose Charles. It turned out to be quite a smart choice.

Saatchi & Saatchi's first account executive (and eighteenth employee) was John Honsinger. The headhunter sent him along for an interview with the less than encouraging advice 'not [to] bother too much'. Saatchis had announced in their *Sunday Times* launch ad that they wouldn't be employing account handlers 'so it would probably never happen'. (The policy rapidly evaporated.)

Honsinger's first interview was with Ron Leagas, and it went well. When Leagas confessed to knowing nothing about the process of getting an ad ready for printing, Honsinger claimed that he did, realizing Leagas wouldn't know what questions to ask him.

Honsinger's next and decisive interview was with the MD at the time, Tim Bell, who fired complex and probing questions about Honsinger's views on the industry. Honsinger, who was struggling, was saved by a combination of the interview being constantly interrupted by people mainly scrounging cigarettes, and Bell's habit of answering his own questions, rendering them entirely and, so far as Honsinger was concerned, helpfully rhetorical. Bell concluded the interview by saying if Honsinger wanted the job he'd have to get out of the habit of calling him 'sir'. Honsinger said, 'Sorry, sir,' for the last time and joined Saatchis.

In the early days, company policy was to hire only tall account handlers, a subtle form of intimidation, designed to 'impress' clients. So no one quite knows how Peter Warren, who had played rugby as a prop in the Saracens' front row and was classic, old-school prop shape, i.e. short and wide, came to be hired.

Several versions of the story are told. In one, Warren was hired by Maurice. On his first day, Warren was seen by Charles who rushed into Maurice's office demanding to know, 'Who's that dwarf I've just seen on the stairs?' Briefly lost for words, the most compelling but tentative rationale Maurice could come up with was,

'He's very clean…'

Warren's own version, recalled by group account director Sue Beazley (formerly Coupland), is that the only reason he got the job was because he was seated when Charles came into the room during his interview, and despite his lack of overall height, Warren is blessed with a very long back apparently, and so seems very tall when sitting down.

Account handler Gareth Coombs recalls his own 'interview' with account director John French, who Coombs describes as 'the trainer of two of our [Saatchis'] MDs, the starter and finisher of two, possibly three, medium-sized agencies, survivor of many heart attacks, advertising expert and bullshitter extraordinaire'. French's first words to Coombs were boomed across the agency's crowded reception. 'The office they've given me is smaller than every room in my house and when I say every room, I'm including bogs and cupboards. I can't insult you by taking you there. We'll go and have lunch.' Over the lunch every subject from Greek myths to rowing and Viking raiders was covered. Every subject apart from advertising. At the end, French, with his spectacular Victorian mutton chop whiskers, announced, 'Well I don't know why, but I like you. The problem is I can't take you on unless Roderick More – I call him Moderate Bore – agrees, and Moderate will hate you.' The outcome of meeting (account director) More was as predicted and French called Coombs to say, 'Well, I was right. He does hate you. He said you had a nasty limp handshake.' A long pause followed, after which French said, 'However, Moderate goes on holiday on Monday, you'd better get yourself over here. I think I can find you a desk.'

French's own recruitment was a little unusual too, according to Sue Beazley. At previous agencies he'd trained both Tim Bell and Roy Warman in media (the two MDs referred to earlier), but after suffering a heart attack he was, according to Beazley, 'on his beam end' without a job. In a kindly and characteristic act, Bell offered French a job in Beazley's group, telling her to 'tuck him away quietly somewhere'. As Beazley discovered though, it was impossible to tuck French away quietly anywhere, clearly demonstrated by Gareth Coombs's first encounter with him. Beazley's own interview took

place in the notorious strip club, Jack's, on Goodge Street, with account supervisor Geoff Culmer asking the questions.

Another recruit, account handler Anne O'Brien, remembers the marathon round of interviews she went through. Two were with Tim Bell who had sent her to see group account director Terry Bannister. 'He wanted to talk to me about problems facing the trade unions, but he didn't offer me a job. Tim had said to come back to him if I didn't get anywhere.'

Bell, shoeless as usual and with lemon yellow socks, sighed and asked what went wrong. 'Nothing,' she said, 'but he didn't have a job for me.' Bell called up Bannister on his 'bink box', a loudspeaker internal 'phone' for senior directors and, without telling Bannister that O'Brien was with him, asked him what he thought of her. Bell watched O'Brien as Bannister said, 'a lot of spunk but no experience'. Bell disappeared, then returned saying they'd offer her a job but he didn't know what or when. He added they needed pretty girls like her – and 'particularly liked the rod of steel he saw as I watched Bannister's assessment of me emerge from the bink box'. And then the interviewing began in earnest. 'Eight interviews later, and vast amounts of gin in each one, Roderick More finally offered me a job.'

Nick Crean's preparation for his interview to be Charles and Maurice's PA was also a little unorthodox. He arrived to find the agency's reception in full party mode, drink flowing. Crean announced he was there for an interview with Maurice and it seemed to him that the whole room then set about preparing him for his meeting by plying him with as many glasses of champagne as possible, before cheering him into the lift for his journey to the top floor. Before the (successful) interview began, Maurice's incumbent PA, Simon Mellor, was dispatched to get Crean a vodka and tonic and an ashtray.

Aside from the unique nature of the interviews themselves, great ingenuity, creativity and occasionally the odd bit of dishonesty has been demonstrated by those looking to secure a job interview at Saatchis. Take William Leach, for example. In 1981, having just graduated, he set about getting a job in advertising. He decided to deliver a letter and his CV personally to the agencies he wanted to join. His older brother's girlfriend told him she and her friends had met someone from Saatchi & Saatchi at a party. It was Paul Bainsfair, and Leach wrote to him asking for a job. Bainsfair replied, saying he'd forwarded his letter to the relevant person, deputy managing director Len Barkey.

Leach called Barkey a couple of weeks later and asked him when his interview was. When Barkey said he didn't know and that interviews were finishing the following day, Leach implied that Bainsfair had promised him an interview. Barkey agreed to squeeze him in. At the interview, Barkey's first question was to ask Leach how he knew Bainsfair. Leach's new-found honesty, when he said, 'I wouldn't know him if he walked through the door right now!' paid off and Barkey put him through to the next round.

Yoram Baumann decided to leave his native Israel to study advertising at Watford College. The final assignment on the course was to prepare a job application. This resulted in Baumann getting an interview at Saatchi & Saatchi. He met Mike Liebling and Tony Dalton who asked him for some sample copy to test his English writing skills. He picked up a book about advertising at the local library, and set about copying a chapter called 'What Makes a Good Account Manager'. He introduced a few spelling and grammatical errors to add authenticity and disguise his wholesale plagiarism, and it worked. He was hired.

On another occasion, a would-be employee turned to very traditional advertising for help. He was spotted walking up and down outside Saatchis' offices in Charlotte Street wearing sandwich boards with the direct message: **'I WANT A JOB'**. The legend of Paul Arnold was born. After a while someone decided it was time to stop ignoring

Paul Arnold's
job application.

Arnold and his enterprising approach to job-seeking, and he was first taken to meet Tim Bell who then passed him on to Terry Bannister. What had emerged pretty quickly was that Arnold had a severe stutter. Nevertheless the interview must have gone well because Bannister offered him a job. No one knows if this was a coincidence or an example of acute cruel irony, but the job Arnold was offered was to work as an account executive on the Penguin biscuit account with its famous campaign line, 'P-P-Pick up a Penguin'.

Not every applicant recognized the need for a little preparation. Andrew Weir blew his first chance of a job as a media assistant at Saatchis. Media group manager Peter Setterington and his colleague Simon Matthews realized early in his interview that Weir didn't have a clue what media was. He was shown the door, being told he was wasting their time. But Weir didn't give up. He wrote to Setterington apologizing for being a time-waster and saying he'd now done his homework and was the right person for the job. No response. He wrote three more letters. Still no response. A fifth letter to Setterington, which began, 'Before I cast aspersions on your parentage…' finally got through. A few days later, media group director Claire Myerscough called him. Her opening words were, 'You're a persistent bastard, aren't you? Why don't you come in for another chat?' Weir was hired and worked at Saatchis for fifteen 'fabulous' years.

Jo de Lapuente, formerly Birrell (who ultimately became an account director), explains how her attempted dishonesty at her third and final graduate trainee interview worked for her. 'Numbers and I didn't get on too well. Fortunately, a rather dull bloke from Durham Uni was sat on my right. I whispered to him, 'If you let me see your answers, I'll buy you a pint afterwards.' To my horror, he raised his hand. One of the interview panel asked him to speak up. He then proceeded to dob me in. What a git. But all the account directors on the panel started to smile. I got the job, he didn't.'

Not all attempts at imaginative job-seeking work out as planned. Receptionist Gill Chapman recalls the creative team who came in to show their work to Paul Arden, the agency's executive

creative director. They called themselves the 'Thunder Jockeys', and for theatrical impact they brought along a small goat. However, the impact was largely on the carpet in reception over which the goat generously distributed its droppings. Arden's PA, Jeanette Marshall, had the thankless task of cleaning up the mess. As Gill notes, **'GOOD JOB SHE WAS AN ANIMAL LOVER.'**

Determination and persistence aren't exclusive to would-be employees. The same qualities have been brought to bear by Saatchi & Saatchi as employers. In one of the most recounted Saatchi stories, Tim Bell was chairman and managing director of the London office and was particularly keen to persuade Jennifer Laing to return to Saatchis. Laing, a very successful – and highly ambitious – group account director had left to join rival agency Leo Burnett to further her career. As then group account director Julian Grandfield points out, Bell's powers of persuasion were legendary, and after a protracted period of wooing, he eventually tabled an exceptional benefits package that included a red Ferrari. Success!

Grandfield adds that such cars were not common amongst her fellow directors at the time and 'considerable envy was inevitable'. However, a footnote to the Ferrari saga comes from group account director Simon De Mille. Apparently Laing called a member of her account group, Peter Buchanan, to say that her new Ferrari was too difficult to reverse out of her drive and 'would he pop round and drive it out for her?'

When highly-rated copywriter Chris Wilkins was hired, his bulging package included a very limited edition white BMW. It was nicknamed 'The Batmobile' because its generous spoilers, widened wheel arches and lowered suspension made it look rather like a bleached version of Batman and Robin's vehicle. Account director Jim Kelly and designer Nick Darke both tell the story of how Wilkins managed to write the car off one day, on London's Park Lane. Apparently, the police officer attending the incident said to Wilkins, 'Nice car, sir. You don't see many of these.'

'No', replied Wilkins proudly, but upside down, 'There are only twelve of them.'

'Eleven, sir,' corrected the police officer.

Saatchi & Saatchi hired a number of different people when the logic wasn't always easy to follow. Paul Arden was famously difficult and famous for being fired (five times before joining Saatchis). But there was no denying what a towering creative talent he was. And it

was this last attribute that guided Charles Saatchi and Jeremy Sinclair to hire him. It was a gamble, but it paid off. Over the fourteen years he was at the agency, Arden steered the place to creative greatness. In a similarly unorthodox move, John Turnbull was hired as a copywriter on the strength of the slim volume of his poetry he presented to Jeremy Sinclair. Turnbull turned out to be an outstanding advertising writer and creative group head, before his sad, untimely death during cardiac surgery.

A poetic hiring.

When Ed Jones took over as creative director of Saatchi's office in Budapest in 1997, he soon decided he needed to refresh the creative department. He'd been creative director in Dubai previously and he'd hired a talented art director there, Darby Roberts. When he put the idea of a move to Budapest to Roberts, he was interested, so a visit to Hungary was arranged.

Roberts got to the agency early in the morning, straight from flying overnight from Dubai. A 'quietly convivial' lunch followed a morning of discussions, first with Jones and then with other agency personnel. The afternoon saw further discussions with more possible future colleagues. As the working day wound down, Jones sent Roberts to a funky bar with some of the agency's creatives.

When Jones joined them an hour or so later, Roberts's Hungarian cultural introduction was well under way. Measures of the local spirit, *pálinka*, had been washed down with beers, and, taking hospitality to another high, some of the creatives had shared with Roberts a few cigarettes, generously loaded with certain exotic aromatic herbs. Jones and Roberts stepped outside so they could have a meaningful discussion about next steps.

Jones takes up the story: 'Darby expressed an extremely positive – if by now somewhat rambling – desire to take the job. He had, after all, been awake for over thirty-six tiring and stressful hours. As I began to outline some aspects of the financial package, Darby suddenly went very pale, crouched forward in spasm and projectile-vomited a couple of Technicolor litres of *pálinka* and beer mixture over my shoes and trousers, at the same time dropping his half-litre glass of beer which exploded on the pavement, adding beer and shards of glass to the vile mixture. I leapt back in horror and disgust. Darby collapsed to his knees, spitting and dribbling. Swaying blearily, and covered in vomit himself, he dragged himself upright and, wiping the repulsive smears from his mouth, asked with a lopsided smile, "Well, did I get the job then?" And of course he did. He was a talented art director.'

Another somewhat unlikely hiring was account director David Miller, who initially seemed determined to scupper any chance he had of working at Saatchis. Tim Bell talked to him about a top marketing job at US pet-food company Ralston Purina. They wanted to launch in the UK, taking on the mighty Mars Petfoods. Miller was less than impressed when he met the boss and reported back to Bell saying the only people who would benefit from the venture would be Saatchi & Saatchi as their advertising agency. 'Don't worry David,' Bell said, 'if it doesn't work out, you can always come and work for us.' To which Miller said, 'What on earth makes

Paul Arden.

you think I'd want to work at a carpet-bagging place like this?' Not perhaps the most endearing, or career-minded, response but three years later with Saatchis having doubled its size and, in Miller's words, 'me having learned respect', Bell got him to join the agency.

A friend of Paul Arden's possibly qualifies for inclusion in the 'dangerous hire' column. Tim Mellors, in an interview with Herman Vaske, says, 'I used to be an addict, an alcoholic and that overtook my nature.' But as with Arden, the only criterion that mattered to Saatchis was Mellors's undisputed creative talent, and he joined the agency's creative department as a copywriter alongside Arden. It's said that either Arden or Jeremy Sinclair offered to pay Mellors's salary out of their own pockets to overcome the initial negative response to his appointment from some sections of the agency. Again, it was an inspired hiring, the groundbreaking 'WHY NOT?' campaign for Lanson champagne being just one example of Mellors's pure creativity.

Why not?   Lanson

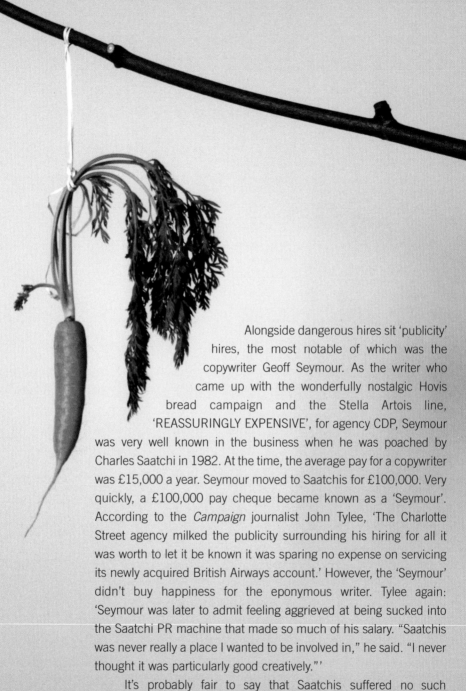

Alongside dangerous hires sit 'publicity' hires, the most notable of which was the copywriter Geoff Seymour. As the writer who came up with the wonderfully nostalgic Hovis bread campaign and the Stella Artois line, 'REASSURINGLY EXPENSIVE', for agency CDP, Seymour was very well known in the business when he was poached by Charles Saatchi in 1982. At the time, the average pay for a copywriter was £15,000 a year. Seymour moved to Saatchis for £100,000. Very quickly, a £100,000 pay cheque became known as a 'Seymour'. According to the *Campaign* journalist John Tylee, 'The Charlotte Street agency milked the publicity surrounding his hiring for all it was worth to let it be known it was sparing no expense on servicing its newly acquired British Airways account.' However, the 'Seymour' didn't buy happiness for the eponymous writer. Tylee again: 'Seymour was later to admit feeling aggrieved at being sucked into the Saatchi PR machine that made so much of his salary. "Saatchis was never really a place I wanted to be involved in," he said. "I never thought it was particularly good creatively."'

It's probably fair to say that Saatchis suffered no such disappointment with their investment.

As Saatchis expanded through acquisition, so their workforce grew. Sean O'Connor recalls how 'the poor staff came over to Lower Regent Street looking like soldiers on the retreat from Moscow…but it was the strength of the Saatchi ethos that made the acquisitions work. People who'd worked in a certain way for years were suddenly liberated by being in such a funny and daring culture…

being taken over by Saatchis was the best thing that had happened to them.'

Right place, right time is probably the twin of round peg, round hole, and one internal appointment that illustrates this is recounted by (then director international) David Welch. 'I was in Germany working with Saatchi's sister agency when late one evening I received a call from Maurice [Saatchi] asking if I would work on the Conservative Party account. Naturally I agreed, but made him aware of the fact that I knew little about politics and loathed and despised every politician I had ever met. He thanked me for agreeing and said that he wanted me on the business because I looked and sounded like a Conservative, but the clincher was I had a blue double-breasted chalk stripe suit.'

For every round peg, round hole appointment, there's a square peg, round hole example. Alex Fynn had been at the same school and in the same year as Charles Saatchi, and knew Maurice 'vaguely'. A chance meeting in the street with Maurice led to Alex being invited to 'come in and see us'.

By Alex's own assessment he had always cocked things up in his career before then. At five previous agencies he'd been 'a smart alec' rather than 'a smart Alex'. He admits that saying the wrong thing at the wrong time was a speciality of his.

Being a committed non-smoker, a non-drinker, keen on exercise and fastidious about his diet meant he wouldn't exactly fit the mould at Saatchis.

However, ahead of his interview Fynn did his homework on the accounts the agency was having difficulties with – the HEC (Health Education Council), and GUS (Great Universal Stores).

Fynn's first interview was with Ron Leagas, who was impressed by his preparation. Leagas spotted Fynn's potential and thought his faith and personality could match clients' needs that were not being fully met. Being Jewish (in the agency at the time only Charles and Maurice were) and having retail advertising experience would fit neatly with GUS. His healthy lifestyle, together with being somewhat pedantic and honest would be a good match for the bureaucracy and mission of the HEC.

But next he saw Tim Bell who was reluctant to accept the credentials Leagas had identified. According to Fynn, Bell wanted 'to expose me and thereby not run the risk of employing a friend of Charles's'. Bell's fear that Fynn would have a direct line to Charles was unfounded, but he began to probe Fynn about his relationship with Charles. Fynn explained how, at school, Charles was always sharing his latest passions with his peers. One of these was rock 'n' roll, and Charles had ignited a love for it in Fynn. 'You're never a rocker!' Bell said.

'Yes I am,' Fynn said.

'All right then,' Bell continued, thinking of a suitably obscure record to test Fynn's claim, 'Who sang "Party Doll"?'

'Buddy Knox', replied Fynn without hesitation.

'Right. You're hired!'

The way Fynn saw it, he was hired because 'I was comparatively honest, very boring and Jewish'. When Fynn arrived as an account director, it was inevitably a culture shock for both parties. John Honsinger describes him as 'one of the brightest people you could wish to meet with a good analytical mind, but he lacked awareness of those around him and you could say he lacked a streetwise approach'. According to Honsinger, Fynn's way of working immediately angered his new colleagues. 'Several people exchanged harsh words with him. For his part, Alex felt that the company was full of unruly, juvenile thugs, and at the end of the first week was ready to quit.' However, ways were found for mutual accommodation. For example, Fynn was thought to be letting the side down by failing to claim expenses high enough to match his colleagues'. So Peter Warren solved the problem quite simply. He forged Fynn's signature on some more appropriately extravagant claim forms.

And it's only fair to record that Fynn himself was not averse to being 'naughty'. He recalls a board meeting where Tim Bell was going on and on, on what Fynn describes as 'a Tim Bell ego trip'. To bring the trip to an end, Fynn decided to 'swim' the length of the boardroom table. It's pleasing to report that in the end, Fynn enjoyed a long and successful twenty-year career at Saatchis, leaving as a deputy chairman.

Andrew Green recalls the somewhat counter-intuitive reasons he was hired as Charles and Maurice's PA. Once he got the job in 1982, he found in his file some handwritten notes from his interview: 'Barbara likes him.' A reference to the receptionist to whom he chatted for about forty minutes while he waited to be called up for his interview. Apparently, the delay was deliberate to see how candidates interacted with other people. 'He smokes.' As Green explains, 'Everybody did – I guess they didn't want a non-smoker sullying the air.' 'Speaks well.' 'Not having a regional accent seems to have been important,' Green says. 'Doesn't know anything about advertising.'

Despite some unconventional and successful hiring practices, Saatchis didn't always rely on such informal and, some would say, random recruitment processes. It became clear by the mid-seventies that clients were looking for account handlers, in particular, who had a more academic, intellectual background. So Len Barkey was made responsible for organizing and running an agency graduate recruitment scheme, which he did for thirteen years. As Barkey confirms, 'Clients themselves were recruiting and training graduates as brand managers and wanted to match them on a like-for-like basis with account handlers.'

Barkey continues, 'We hired our first three graduates in 1977, one of whom, Chris Jones, stayed with the agency until 1984 then went on to agency J. Walter Thompson (JWT), where he eventually became their worldwide chairman and CEO.' Jones's wasn't the only highly successful career launched by the Saatchi graduate recruitment scheme. Several others also went on to become managing directors or to chair major agencies. And many others built very successful careers in and around marketing and advertising.

And at least one, Moray MacLennan, is, at the time of writing, a partner in M&C Saatchi, the breakaway company established by Charles and Maurice in 1995 after they had left the original company.

Barkey points out a key difference between Saatchi's scheme and that of rivals. 'From the beginning, our recruitment strategy had been to trawl as many academic institutions and as many academic disciplines as possible. Some of our competitors chose to focus on Oxbridge, on English, History, Mathematics, even Classics; we went for the people, male or female, with an appreciation of the ultimate nature of the agency business.' To get some idea of the scale of this process, Mike Moszynski points out that over 4,000 applicants a year were competing for a place on the graduate trainee scheme, from which just fifteen people were offered jobs. Moszynski was one and later became an account director.

A filtration system of would-be graduate trainees was devised later when an extremely tough, but appropriate challenge was developed each year. These required great ingenuity and creativity to solve. Gary Sharpen was responsible for creating the challenges. 'Our idea was to make getting an interview as challenging as possible. We figured that by doing this we would discover two things about potential candidates. First, that if they were willing to put the thought, effort and time into applying then it meant they were really hungry for the job, as opposed to simply firing off their CV to countless other agencies. Second, we wanted their response to tell us something unique about them beyond platitudes such as "I'm a passionate team player who thinks outside the box".'

He recalls one of the challenges: 'When graduates contacted the agency to enquire about getting an interview, they were sent a plain black mail pack. Inside was a miniature replica of a portfolio, the sort of thing used by agency people to take creative work to client meetings. On the front of this was a line that read "Do you just want a job in advertising or do you want a job at Saatchis?" As they turned over the pages of the portfolio, a story unfolded. It began "Right, you're about to present a new idea to a client..." The story builds up an increasingly problematic situation, reaching its conclusion with a layout of the idea they had to sell – a version of a Saatchi ad for Club 18–30 that had recently been drawing controversial news coverage for its headline "BEAVER ESPAÑA".

'As if this wasn't challenging enough, it was followed by a postscript which told them one more thing about their client, "Oh, and by the way, he's a born-again Christian". They were then asked to explain how they would set up the idea, how they would present it, and how they would overcome any objections the client might have. The copy signed off with a cheery "Have a nice day". The response was exactly what the agency wanted. There were far fewer applications, but the standard was incredibly high.'

The design of the challenges, to identify applicants with ingenuity and determination, and to weed out the less committed and inventive ones, continued right through to the final one of the series. HR director Kate Morris remembers it. 'It was a digital one where the "click here" box kept moving around so it was really, really difficult, but not impossible to get into the site. They were then told to "enter password here". So we had loads of calls saying they didn't have a password, and so on.' One enterprising Saatchi & Saatchi candidate even demonstrated his ingenuity – and chutzpah – by hacking into the website of Charles and Maurice's new agency, M&C Saatchi, and leaving an appropriately cheeky message. Morris also recalls an unusual aide-memoire used by Alan Bishop (later chairman international) on an interview form he was filling out during a graduate recruitment session. He wrote 'stocking tops'.

The highly talented art director Alan Midgley played an important role in recruiting the best creative talent. 'I cared passionately about getting young people into Saatchis. You win everything with kids. I was advertising assessor at Manchester Poly for five years, together with Maidstone Art College for a similar period. These were two of the best colleges in the country at the time and great production lines. As a result, Saatchis had first pick.'

Hiring the most talented people brings with it the challenge of retention, and there are stories revealing a number of quite diverse

strategies employed by Saatchi & Saatchi to try to keep valued employees. Tim Mellors, who had left Saatchis to take up the creative director role at Publicis, planned to poach the Saatchi art director Digby Atkinson. But when Mellors turned up at Charlotte Street one day with this in mind, he was in for a surprise. Paul Arden, who rated Atkinson very highly, lay in wait for his 'friend' Mellors. He produced two pairs of boxing gloves, and challenged Mellors to fight him for the right to hire Atkinson. Reports suggest Arden landed most of the good punches, but blunt Derbyshireman Mellors's take on it was that Arden 'was pooffin' like a bloody train'.

Boys will be boys

Tim Mellors got slightly more than he bargained for when he turned up at his alma mater, Saatchi and Saatchi, last week with the intention of poaching art director Digby Atkinson.

Any thoughts that Charlotte Street was about to let another of its bright young Turks take the Publicis shilling without a fight were quickly confounded when Saatchis' creative supremo Paul Arden produced two pairs of boxing gloves and challenged the bashful Mellors to stick 'em up.

Observers report that most of the good punches came from Arden, sending Mellors' page boy locks into a state of some disarray. Not that Arden came out of it too well. According to blunt Derbyshireman Mellors: "He was pooffin' like a bloody train."

Arden (left) and Mellors

When Ron Leagas decided to leave Saatchis to form a start-up with Tim Delaney, who was managing director and creative director of the agency BBDO, Ron says, 'Every conceivable offer to tempt me to stay was made, but when Maurice [Saatchi] saw I was unshakeable, he picked up his phone and called my wife. "Jan," he opened in his charming style, "Ron's with me and he's told me of his madcap plan of starting his own agency. I'm concerned for you and your young family and I wondered what I could do to persuade him to stay?" My wife apparently put it to him that he, of all people, should understand the motivation to go it alone. At this, Maurice pulled the company chequebook from his drawer, signed a blank cheque and handed it to me. "Jan," he continued, "what figure would you like Ron to write in the cheque I've just given him to stay?" I don't know to this day what my wife replied, but it was enough to convince him I was beyond persuasion.'

Retaining valuable staff was very important in such a competitive industry. Jeff Stark (copywriter, creative director and then commercials director) had been approached by Dick Hedger of Hedger Mitchell Seymour, to replace Geoff Seymour, and had accepted. Tim Bell asked Stark what it would take to make him stay. 'Double my salary,' Stark said, and Bell agreed. But a year later, Stark left to join Hedger's agency anyway.

However, two years after that, Charles Saatchi called Stark at what had become Hedger Mitchell Stark. 'I want you to come back as creative director,' Charles said.

'I can't,' Stark replied, 'I've got an agency here that depends on me.'

To which Charles said, 'Oh all right – we'll buy the agency. How much do you want for it?' Three and a half million pounds was agreed which, according to Stark, was 'a crazy price since at least half of our billings came from Fosters, which Saatchis would have to resign because it competed with their Castlemaine XXXX account'.

Unlike Stark's experience, for most people, getting a rise at Saatchi & Saatchi was often down to luck and a degree of chutzpah. Digby Atkinson, mentioned earlier, lent Paul Arden a book on a particular photographer. 'After a couple of weeks he returned the book. I took it home that night and was flicking through it when I found a couple of A4 sheets of paper containing the creative department's salary list. Most interesting, thought I! I went into Paul's office the next morning and handed the list over. He went into one of his multidirectional stuttering modes while pacing up and down one side of his huge white desk. I said that no one else had seen it, to which he replied, "No, but YOU have!" Since I knew he was reviewing our salaries I decided to strike while the iron was still warming up. So I took the chance to ask him to double my salary! There followed some more hurrumphing followed by, "Digby – I'll see what I can – I can – do – I'll see..." He did double my salary (less about five grand) and threw in a company car too! Even though I didn't drive.'

Rick Smith, creative director of Saatchi's Sales Promotion Agency, won a pay rise by beating his chairman, Roy Warman, at darts, over the road from the agency at The Carpenters Arms.

Nick Crean remembers asking for a pay rise during his time at Saatchis, and learning a valuable lesson about negotiation in the process: 'I remember asking for a pay rise from £2,500 a year to £3,000 a year. Maurice said, "Ask Martin [Sorrell]," whose office was also on the sixth floor. Martin said, "Ask Maurice," and then said, "Actually no, ask me in another six months." Charles asked why I was looking so downhearted, so I explained. "Bastards," he said, whilst retrieving from his back pocket an eye-watering wad of "petty cash". "Here, have this – and take two hundred cigarettes out of the drawer too. Can't have you upset, I'll sort it."

'Bill Muirhead ambles by and Charles says, "They've tried to do Nick over," and explained what had happened. Bill winks and wanders into Maurice's office and tells him that he wants a pay rise having pulled in BP, BA, Associated Newspapers. Bill was more prepared than I was. "I want £25k a year." Maurice agrees and tells him to clear it with David Perring, the company secretary. Bill says, "Follow me Nick, I'll show you how it's done." Walking into Perring's office, Bill says, "Hi David, Maurice has agreed to put my salary up to £30K! Can you do that mate? Thanks." "See Nick, it's easy, and mate, always include the bonus."'

If the way the company worked was impressive, then Patrick Hanson-Lowe should have been very impressed indeed. In 1984, after a first interview in Charlotte Street with Mark Sinclair, Hanson-Lowe was waiting at Paddington Station for his train back to Bristol. Suddenly, the tannoy blurted out,

'WOULD PATRICK HANSON-LOWE CALL SAATCHI & SAATCHI!'

A pause and then the tannoy message was repeated. He called the agency, went in for a second and final (and successful) interview and was soon working at the place that had impressed him with the chutzpah required to persuade the manager of a major London rail terminus that its message was really urgent, a matter of life and death.

It's alleged that Maurice Saatchi brought a little creativity to recruitment when he and Charles left the company in 1995. Maurice would call a key client and say their account team was about to leave Saatchi & Saatchi and join him in his new venture, so perhaps he would be better off with the new agency too. He would then call the members of the account group and say their client was about to jump ship to his new agency, and if they wanted the chance to carry on working, they'd better join him straight away.

It's worth noting that very, very few people were fired by Saatchis, which could be explained in two ways. One, only the right people were recruited in the first place, and two, those who weren't right tended to leave of their own accord.

Chapter 4

A GREAT SALESMAN WILL ALWAYS DRINK HIS OWN URINE

Achieving the impossible can rely as much on salesmanship as it does on brilliant problem solving, belief and luck. In fact, the success of every business depends, ultimately, on its ability to sell whatever it is it has to offer. And selling skills are all about getting a customer in the right frame of mind to buy.

ADVERTISING EXISTS TO TURN people into buyers. It's the very thing advertising agencies do for a living. But there's one more link in this particular selling chain. Agencies have to persuade their clients to buy their ideas, and when you think about it, there are few things more amorphous or intangible than ideas. But does this make them easier or more difficult to sell than, say, a house? One could argue that houses sell themselves in the sense that it doesn't matter what an estate agent or seller says about a particular property, if it doesn't feel right to the prospective buyer it won't be bought. And here's the nub of it. Pretty much every purchase is driven by emotion. A survey among car buyers once revealed that the deciding factors for choosing one model over another were less to do with rational considerations such as fuel economy and depreciation and more to do with what buyers thought the car said about them, what it did for their self-image and what their peer group would think about them.

In the same way, emotion has a major role to play in whether a client buys an agency's idea or not. For a start, many clients are, by and large, in a discomfort zone when they're judging creative ideas. As marketing people, clients like numbers to support proposals and ventures. Unfortunately, ideas don't come with reassuring numbers, or any numbers for that matter. The fact is, unlike vegetables, the fresher an idea is, the tougher it is likely to be to sell. It's possible to use market research to come up with some numbers to attach to an idea (and provide a protective layer to be worn down the back of one's trousers) but most evidence suggests that market research is the graveyard of originality.

It's an uneasy situation. Agencies are asking people who aren't necessarily creative-minded themselves to buy something creative that isn't even the finished article. There's some unsettling distance between the script on a piece of paper and the commercial on television. The opening phrase to a creative presentation, 'Imagine, if you will…', has a sad and instant redundancy about it, because clients may be very clever at lots of stuff, but being imaginative is less likely to figure anywhere near the top of the list.

For their 1981 Annual Report, Saatchi & Saatchi included the lines of English poet Christopher Logue's 'Come to the Edge' as something of a selling inspiration:

Come to the edge.
We might fall.
Come to the edge.
It's too high!
COME TO THE EDGE!
And they came
And he pushed
And they flew...

The good thing is, clients are human beings. With emotions. A good salesperson knows this and knows, instinctively, how to push the buttons. At the heart of a salesperson's repertoire lie extreme people skills. A Saatchi & Saatchi account handler's response to Richard Myers's observation on a long, foreign location shoot that he seemed to get on really well with the client who was along for the duration, was, 'I can't stand him. But he'll never know.'

A good salesperson knows how to create good relationships, and these in turn create trust. Judging creative ideas may be scary, but it's less scary if the person selling the ideas to you is someone you trust. It can play a pivotal role when it's the agency itself being 'sold' to the client.

When Charles and Maurice were driven out of Saatchi & Saatchi in 1995 as a consequence of a shareholder revolt, there was a risk that the company's biggest client, Procter & Gamble, would leave. Saatchi & Saatchi's worldwide account director for Procter & Gamble was a German called Werner Goerke (sadly no longer with us) and he made it his job to be very close to the client. The client trusted him – so much so that, with the uncertainties of the split, he was asked, along with regional account director Graham Thomas (who supplied this story) to consider how they might leave the agency and run the Procter & Gamble brand's advertising independently.

Goerke and Thomas met up in a New York hotel to decide what to do. They came up with a plan, a proposal for how they might run the business outside the agency. The plan was feasible, but neither of them was prepared to leave the company, which was a condition they had been asked to consider.

Goerke flew to meet Procter & Gamble at their headquarters in Cincinnati to say it wasn't on. While their plan was feasible it would decimate the agency and they were not prepared to trigger that outcome by leaving. The client frequently sought Goerke's advice because they trusted him. In this case, the very future of Saatchi & Saatchi depended on it, and the business was retained. Goerke's unwillingness to put personal gain above loyalty to the agency probably added greatly to the client's already deep trust in him.

Trust played a vital role in the first ever £1 million TV commercial. As account director Annette Crozier (formerly Edwards) recalls, the brief for a new blockbuster commercial for British Airways had been in the agency creative department for some time and people were getting a little twitchy. In fact, by the time a crunch presentation meeting was in the client's diary, the commercial should have already been in production. Working on the brief was a newly hired superstar creative team, art director Graham Fink and copywriter Jeremy Clarke. Their fame, and their reputation for awkwardness, preceded them.

The client meeting was scheduled for 2 p.m. at Heathrow. On the fateful morning there were just two fairly ordinary ideas on the

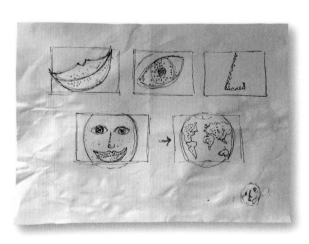

table and nothing from the superstars. However, Edwards received a call from Fink's mobile phone (Fink and Clarke were amongst the first to get their hands on a Dom Joly-style 'brick'). They were in a restaurant but they'd left an idea in their office. It was a rough scribble of a rather grotesque disconnected smiling mouth, an eye, and a nose, and finally a scribbled face.

The British Airways 'Face' commercial. The first TV commercial to cost £1 million to produce.

In the hope of having the idea more fully explained, a call was put through to the 'brick'. Not entirely helpfully, what Edwards learned was that Malcolm McLaren would be doing the music, a feature film director would be needed, and the choreographer of the Los Angeles Olympics' opening ceremony had to be tracked down urgently. Taken together, this was probably not really enough information for the meeting that was looming. Reluctantly, between courses, Fink and Clarke returned to the agency to explain that the shapes were to be formed by people, clothed principally in red, white and blue, coming together to become a smiling face, all to be shot on a majestic, epic scale with an amazing soundtrack, etc.

With the roughest of rough production estimates cobbled together just in time (about £1 million) the presentation team headed for the meeting. Deciding to lead with the two fairly unremarkable ideas, the meeting got off to a less than excellent start when the client, BA's astute advertising manager Derek Dear, expressed disappointment at the quality of both ideas. Although this counted as just about the most hideous insult to a Saatchi & Saatchi team, it served its purpose. It opened the door to present the 'Face' idea. As Edwards explains,

'Apologetically, but with genuine excitement, we craved his indulgence in a roughly executed but potentially massive idea, asking him to see through its lateness to its greatness – and it is to his eternal credit that he did just that. He had been on enough Saatchi journeys from early ideas to finished film, and trusted us sufficiently that he wasn't offended by the style of the paperwork on the table. He saw the potential.'

An iconic commercial was born and appeared on air in 1989. Malcolm McLaren was indeed responsible for the music and Hugh 'Chariots of Fire' Hudson directed it.

Trust, of course, is only one string to a great salesperson's bow. There's flattery and charm, for example, and the high priest of flattery and charm is Tim (now Lord) Bell. When he was Saatchi & Saatchi's managing director he used them to make every employee feel uniquely special, and he used them to similar effect with clients. In Bell's own words,

'There were no lengths to which I wouldn't grovel.'

According to strategic planner Maggie Taylor, Bell's flattery and charm extended to the very top of government. Bell said that Prime Minister Margaret Thatcher's ministers didn't know how to talk to her for the simple reason that she was a woman. By contrast, Bell didn't suffer from the same inhibition. He would freely compliment her on her appearance and would also present her with bouquets of flowers.

The Kenco pack.
Designed at Saatchis
by Nick Darke.

Quick thinking is a prerequisite for successful selling. Although sometimes it's difficult to make out the fine line between quick thinking and being parsimonious with the truth. A pitch for the Kenco coffee business was a case in point. At the time, Denis Norden, who was to star in the commercial, was enjoying huge success as the presenter of *It'll Be Alright on the Night*, the original out-takes and gaffs TV show. The client loved the idea but, reflecting on Norden's current stardom, thought his fee might be too high. Sensing the idea – and the business – slipping away, Bell didn't miss a beat. He told the client not to worry because he knew Denis Norden well – in fact, he'd just got his daughter a job at Capital Radio. He said Norden would probably do it for a year's supply of coffee or something like that.

With these reassuring noises, the business was won. Norden's agent negotiated a three-year deal worth about £150,000, a very significant amount of money at the time. The agency presented the budget to the client with Norden's massive fee included but as camouflaged as possible. The chairman of Kenco said, 'I can't understand why this seems so expensive.' No amount of TV production flimflam and bullshit could keep a lid on the chairman's inevitable, and dreaded, question: 'So how much is Denis Norden getting, then?' In little more than a whisper, the chairman got his

answer: '£150,000'. A pregnant pause. At the end of which the chairman observed, 'He drinks a fuck of a lot of coffee, doesn't he?'

Great salespeople are blessed with more than their fair share of intuition. This was very valuable when it came to negotiating the fee a client would pay for the agency's services. As Tim Bell observes, when fees replaced the old media commission system by which agencies earned their income, there was no formula for calculating them. There was a modicum of logic applied, for example the size of the account, but by and large it was down to raw intuition and a certain amount of nerve and brinkmanship. Bell explains that a figure would be proposed, say £10k, and judging by the client's reaction, the 'salesman' would instantly sense if the figure needed to be reduced a little for an agreement to be reached.

Tim Bell wasn't alone at Saatchis in being acutely intuitive when it came to fees. Neil Kennedy worked at Dorlands when it was sold to Saatchi & Saatchi in 1981. He asked a Saatchi director how the agency charged. The director said, 'We use the blink system.' Kennedy asked to be enlightened and was told that after winning a pitch, when the client asked how much, he would always reply, '£100k,' and if the client didn't blink, he'd say, '...a month'.

Being somewhat parsimonious with the truth occasionally merges elegantly with the principle that necessity is the mother of invention, as Maurice Saatchi clearly demonstrated. Phillippe Cordonnier was the CEO of Saatchi's Belgian office. The agency, acting independently and ignoring any potential commercial fallout, decided to run an ad urging the people of Belgium to demand that

Lord Stokes, then boss of Saatchi London's client British Leyland, did not carry out his threat to stop producing the Mini at their major factory in Belgium. Stokes was furious, which inspired Maurice Saatchi to write to him informing him that Cordonnier had gone mad and, as a consequence, had placed himself voluntarily in the hands of a psychiatrist.

Paul Bainsfair, as a group account director, led Saatchi's pitch for British Steel's privatization campaign. 'We were competing against four other agencies, and although we pitched the best work we had, you'd have to say that, by Saatchi standards, it was only an average pitch. The next day the client called with the bad news. He was sorry but we hadn't made it through to the next round.

With some trepidation, I went to tell Paul Arden (executive creative director) what had happened. Arden, not unusually, threw a fit and screamed at me, demanding to know what I was going to do about it.' Bainsfair admits to not having a clue what to do until, late in the day, inspiration or recklessness struck him. 'I phoned the client and said, "Something awful has happened. I made a terrible mistake. We had two campaigns and I brought along and presented the wrong one! May we please come back tomorrow morning and present the right one?"

"It's most unusual," the client said, "but OK, we'll give you the chance to show us the correct one."

'I then told my team about presenting the other campaign the next day. "What other campaign?" they asked.

"The one the creatives are going to come up with overnight," I said. They worked all night and the "correct" campaign won us the business.'

Saatchi & Saatchi copywriter Eugene Ruane believes the best salesman he ever worked with 'by a mile' was Kim Wicksteed of Saatchi & Saatchi New Zealand's Wellington office (Wicksteed would eventually become CEO of Saatchis New Zealand). Ruane and his creative partner, art director Maggie Mouat, were given a new business pitch to work on. It was a share issue for a government-owned power company.

By Ruane's own admission, the work they produced wasn't very exciting. The legal people saw to that apparently. It may explain why, at the pitch meeting, the client didn't seem to care about the creative work and was only interested in the costs. Specifically, he wanted to know why Saatchi & Saatchi was charging twice as much as the next closest competing agency. Cue a broadly smiling Kim Wicksteed who answered, 'Because we can do it and they can't.' When the client asked Wicksteed to explain what he meant, he said, 'We've handled eight out of ten of these share issues in New Zealand in the past five years. All of ours have been oversubscribed. The two we weren't involved in were undersubscribed.' He went on, 'In fact I know that some of those who were involved in choosing what turned out to be the wrong agency actually lost their jobs because of it. The fact is, if we lose, we just lose a bit of cash. If you lose…well, let's say, I don't think the government will be too happy with some of you.' At this point, with the clients slightly stunned, the agency leaves and heads off for some lunch.

Returning to the agency around 5 p.m., the phone rings. Saatchi & Saatchi has been awarded the account. Some might call that scare tactics. Others would see it as persuasion through observation.

And then there's the power of a little emotional blackmail. One of the most famous television commercials of the 1980s in the UK was Saatchi & Saatchi's 'Furry Friends' spot for the Solid Fuel Advisory Council (see Chapter 6). Three members of the Saatchi & Saatchi team involved in this account left the company to form a breakaway agency. Paul Cowan, Adrian Kemsley and Maggie Taylor immediately tried to take the Solid Fuel business. For legal reasons, if they were successful, they would have to come up with an entirely new campaign.

At the re-pitch to keep the business, Saatchi & Saatchi's MD at the time, Pete Watkins, walked into the meeting with the dog from the much-loved commercial and simply asked the clients if they would be happy to make the old boy redundant. It worked. Saatchi & Saatchi retained the business. And saved Cowan, Kemsley and Taylor the bother of having to come up with a new idea.

There are, of course, occasions where blunt, brutal truth wins the day. Account director Tim Nicholls recalls having a furious row in the pub with a client who was insisting on moving some of his media budget into radio. To resolve the impasse, Nichols called over the account's media expert who was also in the pub, and asked him to explain to the client why radio was wrong for his brand. Without hesitation, but with complete certainty he said, 'Radio is shit.' The money stayed on TV.

Group account director Tony Dalton prepared this same recipe for a showdown meeting with Black & Decker. The account was new to the agency but the honeymoon period had been extremely short. They'd rejected all the TV commercial scripts written for them. Dalton decided something had to be done. He assembled three of Black & Decker's marketing managers in his office and quickly removed the clients' smiles and silenced their giggles with this broadside: 'Your account has been in this agency for only a few weeks and it's already a joke account around here. And I'll tell you why. It's because you're acting like a bunch of cunts.' One of the clients was so surprised he fell off the end of the armless sofa he was sitting on and landed on the office floor. But the showdown did the trick. Black & Decker went on to become one of the agency's most rewarding accounts, and the advertising created for them won numerous awards. Tony Dalton was even invited to attend their board meetings.

In a similar vein, agency client Mars were thinking about changing the name of their Marathon bar to Snickers, in the interests of conformity, or efficiency across Europe. A difficult call, and the agency was asked to address the issue. According to Pete Watkins, 'Mars expected work to be done. Research. Analysis. Deep thinking. A long and reasoned response. The response in fact was a letter which said something along the lines of, "The fact that you've asked us the question means that you must know the answer. Do it."'

Needless to say, honesty can often be a double-edged sword and there is a real danger in allowing honesty (and possibly any creatives) to enter into a debate. In another meeting with Mars, copywriter Harry Shaw remembers, 'The late, great creative director Andy Rork got exasperated at a Mars meeting and said to the gathering of eminent clients, "Come on, it's only a chocolate bar!" He was never allowed to attend a Mars meeting again.'

In the right situation, of course, a well-timed bit of honesty can engender trust and win the day. At one stage the Toyota account was looking shaky and Trevor Taylor, the general manager of Toyota GB, was becoming increasingly disappointed with the quality of the Saatchi creative ideas his marketing team was presenting to him. In fact, it was his marketing team that were rejecting good Saatchi ideas and steering the agency towards the more mundane work that they then took to Taylor. At the time, Adam Crozier was the agency's media director but, for some reason, he was given the job of saving the Toyota account.

A meeting was set up with Taylor. It was felt that Crozier needed added status to help him along, so he was immediately promoted to vice chairman. But early in the meeting Crozier had an attack of honesty. In rapid succession he told Taylor about his instant vice chairmanship and that he knew very little about cars. Honesty might be seen as a rather quaint policy, but it seems to have been the key to a successful meeting. Crozier had also taken along all the good work that had been rejected, and Taylor loved it. Crozier's argument, that while he knew little about cars, Taylor's team obviously knew nothing about advertising, convinced Taylor to keep the Toyota account at the agency.

When blunt, brutal truth has the element of surprise added to it, the outcome can be very pleasing indeed.

John Honsinger recalls an instance involving group financial director (later Sir) Martin Sorrell that employed just this tactic: 'In 1982, Martin Sorrell introduced me to a City friend who subsequently became a client of mine at (Saatchis subsidiary) The Sales Promotion Agency. The client was an investment bank, and after working with them, some money was outstanding. At a monthly meeting, Martin asked why it hadn't been paid. I explained there was no good reason, so he picked up the phone to speak to the chairman of the bank. He forced him out of a board meeting, explained that he was with me listening in, and wanted to know why the bill had not been paid. The chairman was annoyed and said he had to get back to his board meeting and would deal with the matter later. In response, Martin told him in no uncertain terms that he would not let him leave the conversation until he promised to pay the full amount in the next twenty-four hours. Threats were made on both sides and Martin came out on top by warning that he would ruin the chairman's reputation if he did not comply. The money was paid and obviously we lost the business. Martin told me afterwards that it didn't matter that we were the supplier, in business no one respected you unless you stood up for yourself.'

The persuasive power of brutal brevity is matched, at the other end of the spectrum, by careful extended groundwork. Saatchi & Saatchi Wellington had written a TV commercial script for the Toyota HiLux ute. The visuals were a series of things going wrong as a consequence of the HiLux's extra power. The script had just one word in it. Kim Thorp, the agency's executive creative director at the time, picks up the story, starting with that one word:

Bugger.

'No, not the deep dark meaning involving priests and young boys, but the colloquial expression that had grown throughout New Zealand. We understood the risks, two years' worth of the production money for Toyota's top selling HiLux ute – we knew that it could be off air within days of it launching. Bugger. But we had done our homework. Been to see the Television Commercials Approval Bureau. They gave it the tick. And canvassed most of the members of the Broadcasting Complaints Board, over a beer, one at a time, and quietly dealt with their issues and any resistance they might have. Everything we had was riding on one word. Bob Field, Toyota CEO, loved it. Approved it in moments. Then the assurance – it has to last all of two years, not two minutes!

It was the most complained about commercial of all time. Hundreds of well-intentioned Kiwis howled their disgust that something so dreadful could be on our screens. Even though it wasn't screened until after 8.30 p.m. But miraculously the Complaints Board held firm and adjudicated that it was part of the common

Kiwi vernacular, and their decision made front-page headlines in Wellington's *Evening Post*. And then like an epidemic, bugger could be heard everywhere: golf courses, workplaces and parties. Non-Toyota utes sported bugger on their spare-wheel covers. New Zealand fell in love with the commercial and kept it in the number-one favourite position in TV viewer polls for over six months. And it was universally awarded around the world.'

Careful preparation is matched for effective selling by persistence. The essence of persistence is saying 'no' to 'no', over and over again if necessary. In the UK, Saatchi & Saatchi won the Hi-Tec sports footwear business after it had already been awarded to a competing agency.

The creative idea Saatchi & Saatchi pitched revolved around the line, 'SHOES FOR YOUR HEAD' and featured photographs of sports stars with, er, Hi-Tec shoes on their heads. Pete Watkins led the pitch and was seriously miffed when JWT won. He decided the agency should hound the client – into a change of heart, hopefully. The agency produced a double-page spread ad of Chelmsford City Football Club players wearing their Hi-Tec boots on their heads. The ad was inserted into fifty copies of the *London Evening Standard* newspaper, and one of the copies was presented to a startled client as he left an investors' meeting in the City. The client happened to be chairman of the football club. He granted the agency another meeting where he ripped up the JWT contract and signed Saatchi & Saatchi's saying, 'I've got to appoint you. If I don't, you'll work with my competitors.'

Toyota UK's marketing director Graham Smith's straightforward and somewhat discouraging response to the script he'd just had presented to him for the launch of the RAV 4 was, 'Over my dead body.' Saying 'no' to the client's very definite 'no' in this case, the agency decided that a little ad hoc research might help their cause. They tested the idea against the target audience, and they loved it. On hearing this, Smith's response showed what an outstanding marketer he was. 'I don't like it,' he said, 'but the people we're trying to sell to do like it, so we'll go ahead with it.'

Persistence was required when Saatchis were briefed by their Sony client to create a launch campaign for the blockbuster movie, *Godzilla*. The client wanted the usual posters, press and movie

Guerrilla advertising for *Godzilla*, seen here in London's Tottenham Court Road.

trailers package, but creative director Gary Sharpen and his team saw an opportunity to do something very different. 'We wondered what city streets would look like if *Godzilla* had actually paid a visit,' says Sharpen. 'In the dead of night, a few days before the movie was to premiere, we dumped cars all over London. These cars had been well and truly trashed. Having been sourced from an old-school wrecking yard they had been flattened – this gave the impression of having been trod on by the monster. These wrecked cars were covered in emergency services-style tape carrying just the words "!!!ALERT!!! GODZILLA" Deliberately, there was no other branding and no mention of it promoting the film.'

Londoners awoke to the carnage of the monster. The *Evening Standard* newspaper reported it generously, while Capital Radio and Classic FM presenters talked about it on air. The media coverage it generated was literally priceless. Interestingly though, when we first presented the idea to the client it was largely dismissed for not being what they were used to, being perceived as complicated to achieve and expensive to produce. And here's where persistence kicked in. 'Over the next six weeks, we kept bringing up the idea at subsequent client meetings. We also charged a junior, but tenacious, account executive with reminding the client about it at every opportunity. We showed how we could execute it and do so at a very modest cost for a film launch. About ten days before the film premiere the client just told us to get on and do it. After seeing the publicity it generated, he said,

"Now I know why I have an agency."'

Occasionally, outside events can interrupt a salesperson's flow and this calls for a different kind of persistence. David Palmer was the senior account handler for a supermarket chain in Saudi Arabia. According to Ed Jones, the agency's creative director in Saudi at the time, 'Palmer wasn't a typical streetwise Saatchi & Saatchi account man. Well over six feet tall and built on a generous scale, he had been to Gordonstoun School at the same time as the Prince of Wales. In Riyadh to present the crucial winter campaign to the marketing director, Palmer had taken the client through the opening part of the presentation, the TV spots, and was about to continue with the outdoor work when, with a thunderous roar, the windows suddenly exploded inwards, shards of glass sprayed into the room, the shredded blinds lashed like corn in a storm, the false ceiling collapsed in a fine powder, the floor rose and fell like a fairground cake walk, the furniture in the room slid in all directions, and a deafening cacophony of car alarms broke out.

'It turned out later that Al Qaeda had exploded two truck bombs at the US-operated Saudi National Guard training centre, located about a hundred metres away across the car park. For a few moments, as they tried to comprehend what had happened, David and his client stared at each other, frozen, aghast and in shock, as a blizzard of fine plaster dust settled gently upon them. Then, calling upon the discipline engendered by years of cold baths and cross-country runs in the freezing Scottish countryside, Palmer stirred himself: "So, moving on to the outdoor ads..."'

When Palmer returned to the agency's Jeddah office, he recounted his extraordinary experience to his colleagues. When he'd finished, Jones admits saying, 'Never mind all that, Palmer, did you sell the bloody ads?' According to Jones, 'Palmer breathed in and drew himself up to his full six feet four inches. He paused and then, with a curled lip of contempt at the very suggestion he might have failed, said, "Of course!"'

When does persistence turn into irritation and annoyance, before eventually reaching irreversible rejection? Great salespeople just know where that line lies. And selling sometimes calls for pure opportunism. Copywriter Harry Shaw recalls selling a script for a *Sunday Times* commercial, featuring a story about the actor Alec

Guinness, to the then editor Andrew Neil, who was notoriously difficult to get to. However, Shaw and Neil were both members of the RAC club in London's Pall Mall. Shaw and Neil were both swimming. When Neil left the pool, Shaw followed him into the hot showers and presented the script verbally in a place Neil couldn't escape from, and where he couldn't answer his phone. He approved the script and it went on to be an award winner.

Strategic planner Sylvia Meli recalls another story of opportunism with a difficult-to-get-to client, in this case, Hewlett Packard: 'A newly promoted Saatchi & Saatchi account manager, Jeremy Scarfe, was given the job of selling a campaign for a new All-in-One printer. The client said he was too busy to see Scarfe on the day requested. Deadlines were looming, but the client insisted he was too busy. He was so busy, he said, he hardly had the time to have his hair cut. A-ha! Scarfe spotted his opportunity. He jumped on a flight to Stuttgart with the creative work. He sold the campaign successfully, but did admit having had some difficulty getting the boards on which the ads were mounted correctly angled in the opposing mirror for the client to see them because the hairdresser kept getting in the way.'

Opportunism can be a simple case of reading a situation correctly. Ron Leagas, Saatchi's managing director at the time, recalls how the airline British Caledonian had a marketing director who liked to keep the agency on its toes by periodically threatening to fire them. Sometimes there was a good reason, but usually it was about squeezing even more service out of the agency – or just a good lunch. One particularly good lunch with the agency's then media director, Roy Warman, wasn't enough to secure a reprieve and when they returned to the agency, Warman asked Leagas to join them in reception. Leagas quickly realized, after a couple of questions to the client, that the threat was neither logical nor, he judged, able to be carried out 'if the discussion was elevated'. But Leagas decided, given the client's post-lunch state (and despite his superior size), not to elevate but to lower the debate. He challenged the client to an arm wrestle right there in reception. If the client won, he could carry out his threat, and if Leagas won, the agency got to retain the business. Leagas, the opportunist, won.

At times there's no substitute for sheer nerve. David Miller was the group account director responsible for the tiny UK Campbell's Soup account, but the Saatchi brothers thought the agency deserved more of their business in the US. Miller's tale is that the incredibly well-connected Simon Parker-Bowles, who had already successfully introduced Charles and Maurice to Lord King, the chairman of British Airways, set up a meeting with Campbell's at their worldwide headquarters in Camden, New Jersey. More specifically, the meeting was with Herb Baum, the worldwide head of marketing for Campbell's Soup. He'd been told by Parker-Bowles that a bunch of senior Saatchi people (including Miller) happened to be passing through Camden and would like to pay him a courtesy visit. Over a lunch of Campbell's soup, followed by Campbell's meatballs accompanied by tap water, Baum masked his scepticism about the agency's visit (no one happens to pass through Camden). The agency left empty-handed, of course, but not long afterwards, Saatchi & Saatchi London was appointed to handle the enormous Campbell's V8 business in the US.

The Saatchi & Saatchi agency in Spain also showed a certain degree of nerve and some impressive salesmanship when they embarked on a project to promote the new Lovemarks initiative.

One for Stanley Gibbons.

Lovemarks was the invention of worldwide CEO Kevin Roberts to describe the heightened loyalty consumers have to certain brands. And a loyalty Saatchi & Saatchi could generate through the quality of its creative communications. Saatchi & Saatchi EMEA marketing director Micky Denehy says the agency designed a Saatchi & Saatchi Lovemarks postage stamp and 'the account team got the Spanish Post Office to accept it as a legal stamp, so, from then on, every letter leaving the agency had a legal tender Lovemarks stamp on it!'

A popular synonym for chutzpah is balls. And few Saatchi people have ever been better endowed than Jennifer Laing. During her time as an account director, according to account man Patrick Hanson-Lowe, she entered the exceedingly macho world of Wimpey Homes to pitch for the £20 million business and 'almost single-handedly' won it. She charmed them with insight and the belief that they could be more than just a builder. It's said she was the first ever woman to enter their boardroom.

Later, when Laing became chairman (yes, chairMAN – she insisted) of the London agency after the split in the mid-1990s, she was made aware that the Conservative Party owed the agency around £1 million. She and the holding company's financial director Charlie Scott set up a meeting with Lord (Philip) Harris (aka The Carpet King because of his fifty years of experience in carpet retailing), the deputy chairman of the Conservative Party Board of Treasurers. The conversation was civilized, but Harris made the mistake of showing off, with considerable pride, a rather flash ormolu clock he had newly acquired whilst, at the same time, suggesting the party had no money. 'You can give us the clock then!' said Laing. The party paid up.

Over in Los Angeles, the Saatchi agency Team One (set up initially by Saatchi & Saatchi to handle the launch of Lexus in the US) came up with a cunning stunt to win the Savoy Pictures studio account. The movie industry is an insider's industry, and Team One was an outsider, so it was always going to be a tricky move. As Joe Cronin, the agency's then worldwide account director for Toyota, based in LA, describes it, 'Savoy wanted support and involvement from Saatchi & Saatchi New York.' So Team One engaged Bob Kennedy, who was then vice chairman of Saatchi & Saatchi North America, to be the New York representative on the account.

Come the pitch and the Savoy clients were told that Kennedy, at the appropriate moment, would be joining the meeting in LA via the very recently introduced satellite TV link. When contact was made with Kennedy in New York, a very snowy image lasted only long enough for him to say, 'Whenever you need me, I'll...', at which point the link disappeared, which was not unusual at the time.

WHENEVER YOU NEED ME...

But then, suddenly, Bob walked into the meeting room in LA with the words, 'As I was saying, whenever you need me, I'll be there.' The president of

...I'LL BE THERE!

Savoy Pictures looked across the table at the agency, put his finger to his mouth indicating he'd been hooked. Theatre works as a selling tool because it demonstrates the agency is capable of ingenuity and daring. It also shows the agency cares.

John Wright, who was a management supervisor in the London agency, is a big believer in passion and demonstrated belief, and thinks it's the key to successful selling. He certainly went the extra mile to persuade Toyota's commercial director, Mike Moran, to buy a print ad for the Toyota Land Cruiser.

The Land Cruiser was, and still is, the vehicle trusted by most drivers in deserts throughout the world not to let them down. Anecdotally, in these kinds of environments, drivers who break down resort to drinking their own urine to survive. So the ad's headline was, 'HERE'S TO NEVER HAVING TO DRINK YOUR OWN URINE.' Moran loved the idea but was concerned that it would cause offence. No amount of carefully crafted rational argument was getting him to change his mind. Eventually, realizing that rational was being about as effective as an ashtray on a motorbike, Wright came up with an idea that was splendidly irrational but apposite, outrageous but a clear demonstration of his, and the agency's, belief in the ad. Wright's proposal was that if Moran approved the ad, he, Wright, would drink his own urine. 'Disgusting!' said Moran. 'I'll do it now!' said Wright. But Moran wasn't persuaded by the offer. At the end of the meeting, Wright made it clear his proposal stood.

Shortly afterwards, Wright went on holiday and was unaware of the success of the Toyota pitch. When he returned he was in another Toyota meeting with Moran, unrelated to the Land Cruiser ad. During the meeting Moran excused himself and came back with a cocktail glass in his hand and a magazine under his arm. He opened the magazine, *Lumberjack Monthly*, to show Wright a double-page spread advertisement: the Land Cruiser urine ad. 'Your turn,' said Moran. He insisted on accompanying Wright to the men's room to witness a cocktail shaker being put to uncommon use by Wright. Ice was added and both Wright and Moran ceremoniously gave Wright's self-brewed beverage a good shake. And then Wright went right ahead with his side of the bargain and drank his own urine. A great salesperson will do whatever it takes to make a sale. Because it goes beyond being just a job. It's a matter of honour.

Chapter 5

DON'T JUST DO IT, DO IT FIRST

There may be a fine line between brave and foolish, but the gulf between first and also-ran is immeasurably wide.

AN INTERVIEWER ONCE SUGGESTED to Ron Dennis of the McLaren Formula 1 racing team that they must be very pleased with the second place they'd just taken in a particular Grand Prix. Dennis replied, 'No we're not! We were the first of the losers!' And who wants to be a loser? Who wants to be an also-ran? It's said that the worst Olympic medal to win is silver, not bronze. So near, yet so far. And the worst place to come in an Olympic event is fourth. Again, so near, yet so far.

There's a difference, however, between coming first and being the first to do something. Coming first can be down simply to being more talented. Or being luckier. Or to sheer hard work. But being the first to do something calls for a pioneering spirit. Having little respect for the status quo. A willingness to break new ground, to break rules. And ultimately having no fear of failure. It takes daring. It takes ambition. It takes chutzpah.

Even their harshest critics would not deny that Saatchi & Saatchi are pioneers. The full-page advertisement Saatchi & Saatchi ran in *The Sunday Times* in the UK on 13 September 1970, announced their arrival. It was also a statement of intent, and an indication of their view of the world. 'WHY I THINK IT'S TIME FOR A NEW KIND OF ADVERTISING' was the headline, followed by long columns of well-researched, well-written, thoughtful and thought-provoking copy. The byline names Jeremy Sinclair, the agency's creative director. According to Sir John Hegarty, however, the ad was written by Bob Heller, the editor of *Management Today* magazine.

But authorship matters much less than content. Two sentences in particular come close to representing the foundation stones of Saatchi & Saatchi's creative approach. 'Great advertising nearly always involves looking at a marketing problem in a totally new light – often from a viewpoint which is distasteful to the conventional client' was one. The other was the observation that

'Wasted ads are the ones which nobody sees, reads or notes.'

The advertisement was surprising in many ways. It positioned Saatchi & Saatchi as intelligent and measured, but revolutionary at the same time. What it had to say would have interested staid captains of industry and fiery ambitious creatives alike. It also distanced the company from established agencies.

Why I think it's time for a new kind of advertising.

By Jeremy Sinclair

The first Lord Leverhulme, Britain's original margarine and soap king, won undying literary fame by observing that half of the money which he spent on advertising was wasted, but that he didn't know which half. For all he knew, Lord Leverhulme may have wasted still more of his advertising money, and many of today's advertisers doubtless waste more than Lord Leverhulme.

Wasted ads are the ones which nobody sees, reads or notes. Ads are unseen unless the agencies which create and place them, and the clients who approve and pay for them, remember the prime purpose of advertising. Lord Leverhulme never forgot that prime objective. In his day, the age of the entrepreneur, the great ads and the great advertisers were the great sellers. They still are.

Expenditure of shareholders' money is only justified if it ultimately produces a quantifiable and adequate return in the same terms – money. In advertising language, this means that a campaign only succeeds if it ultimately helps to create new sales for the client, and does so effectively and economically. This self-evident truth rests on another: advertising cannot create sales unless (first and above all) it catches the consumer's attention; then, interests the consumer; then, changes the consumer's attitudes; and finally, sells to the consumer. These are the four Stages of Man in advertising; Attention, Interest, Desire and Action.

The sheer power of advertising is so great, anyway, that it can triumph over a lack of penetration which would kill off many other industries. Research by Gallup shows that only 26 per cent of readers of a national newspaper read the average *full page* ad: in other words, if the ad pulls, it does so despite the 74 per cent of the readership which completely ignores the advertiser's expensive message, and which never passes advertising's Stage One. Gallup's files also contain examples of full-page full colour ads in a national daily which were noted by only 5 per cent of the readers, and actually read by none of them. Plainly, an ad which everybody reads is far superior to one which somebody reads: but an ad which nobody reads does nothing except cost money. Oddly enough, some companies expect little else from their advertising.

A familiar management failing ...

This emerged from a recent survey in *Management Today* by Simon Majaro, director of Strategic Management Learning, and a partner with management consultants, Urwick Orr. He found that many manufacturing firms glibly claimed advertising objectives (making no attempt to measure their achievement) like "improving image of company's products", "improving company's image" and "creating brand awareness" – these objectives were put above "increasing sales", which was regarded as somehow inferior. This is an example of a familiar management failing– putting the means before the end.

Images and brand awareness are meaningless if they fail to achieve greater turnover: the test is the cash in the till, and passing that test is far harder than image-building or winning awards. The great split between the so-called creative hot shops and the big marketing agencies is wholly fictitious. A creative ad is only an exercise in self-indulgence unless it achieves the client's marketing purposes, expressed in concrete terms of sales penetration; and a marketing agency cannot achieve any result, except the expensive duplication of its clients' own marketing and merchandising skills, unless it creates ads that seize the public mind.

The proper role of the middle-man

The self-induced schizophrenia in the advertising world can create confusion in the agency itself. For example, what is the proper role of the account executive, the middleman between the advertiser and the people who are paid to create the ads? It must not be to block the creators from direct access to the client: for the risk then is that ads will get created, not to sell more *for* the client, but to give the middle-man something which he can sell *to* the client.

The current experiments with internal agency organisation point to this anxiety: the famous open plan offices at KMP, with creative people hopefully jostling against account executives to some better effect than bruised shoulders; or the division of Lonsdale Crowther into self-contained groups of creative and account-servicing staff; or the total abolition of the account executive by the new Saatchi and Saatchi agency, which adds to its gratifying start of almost £1 million of initial billings, a self-declared role as "just salesmen". The account executive's replacement is a co-ordinator who is not briefed by the client, does not brief the creative people, does not pass judgment on ads and does not present ads to the client, but works with the creators as a day-to-day administrator.

Obviously, the mode of organisation counts for nothing compared to the results and, in the agency world, there is always a fashion of not being in fashion. No new agency, bursting with all the usual bravado would dream of appearing without new organisational clothes. The Saatchi and Saatchi salesmanship dress gets its individual cut (what you might call a Unique Selling Proposition) from the peculiar nature of its birthplace – a hard-selling creative consultancy called Cramer Saatchi.

Two years ago, creative consultancy itself was a virgin idea. Its subsequent flowering also points to problems inside the big agency. An agency presumably calls in consultants because of doubts whether its own creative staff can produce effective advertising unaided. Several causes arise naturally from time to time even in the best-regulated shops like simple shortage of able bodies; or else thinking on an account gets too inbred, until the agency realises it cannot judge campaigns objectively – it is trapped by its total immersion in the client's own business philosophy and prejudices.

Great advertising nearly always involves looking at a marketing problem in a totally new light – often from a viewpoint which is distasteful to the conventional client. Thus Bill Bernbach of Doyle Dane Bernbach came back to Avis with the unwholesome news that the only thing which the agency could find to say about Avis was that it was Number Two: the rest is advertising (and selling) history. The consultant trades on his blissful ignorance – on coming in fresh to every account, unexposed to the client's sales objectives, marketing problems, management preoccupations and fixed ideas.

Diminishing the power of the retail chains

The major snag when consultants, like Saatchi and Saatchi, proliferate into agency form, is how to preserve this freshness. Their device is to split the agency into two groups on every campaign. The so-called working group, advised by an ex-supermarketeer whose role is to tilt at the growing power of the big retail chains, gets fully involved with the client; its Siamese twin, the control group, knows nothing about the marketing ideas behind the campaign, and asks only one awkward question. Will these ads sell to a consumer who knows equally little about the marketing logic behind them and cares even less?

The potential for what is euphemistically known as "creative tension" between the groups is enormous, but again the results are the only criterion. For this particular agency, that criterion looms especially large, since it is not cheap – charges will average about 22 per cent of total billings – far above the norm: it results from dropping that dear, dying, illogical commission system in favour of cost-plus fees. Its clients pay the agency's costs, amortised over the period of expenditure and net of commission; the quid pro quo for the 22 per cent touch is a promise of the cheapest possible buying of space and time. The growth of the new media brokers has shown how far shrewd and determined media buying can stretch a budget (and stretch a middle-man's profit).

The mechanical task of placing ads most effectively, in terms of price and impact, has been most curiously neglected. For instance, back covers of magazines are seen by far more people than inside pages: yet all media owners know that most back covers are hard to sell. Advertising is beset by other hoary prejudices – for instance, that there's no point in advertising in August and January. Prevalence of myths, which could be smartly destroyed by investigation (or even by common sense), means a disregard for fact – and fact is the foundation of all successful advertising.

A salesman's job

You cannot, except for the briefest span of time, persuade consumers to buy a bad product. If the product is genuinely good, the most effective method of selling and advertising that product is invariably to present the facts about its advantages. Advertising which does its salesman's job presents accurate, meaningful facts about the goods or services of the client: and these few factual ads must be bold or original enough to persuade readers or viewers to pay attention to the facts.

Similarly, effective advertisers must judge agencies by the facts of their own sales performance – and many don't: Saatchi and Saatchi make the unlikely boast that their salesmanship line will cut them off from half their potential clients. Certainly, it is folly to hide behind the smokescreen of Lord Leverhulme's celebrated dictum (another non-factual myth) and the intangibles of the image. What should concern all advertisers are the tangibles of their advertising expenditure and of the revenue which that spending generates – or (as in the Case of the Wasted Ads) fails to generate.

Saatchi & Saatchi and Company

6, Golden Square, London, W1R 3AE.

01-734 9111

Of course, the proof of Saatchi & Saatchi's manifesto was in its delivery. And right from the start Saatchi & Saatchi set about overturning existing advertising categories and creating new ones. One category to get the Saatchi treatment early on was public service announcements. Up to that time they'd been pretty dull and polite. 'Coughs and Sneezes Spread Diseases' was probably the most creative there had been. But Saatchi & Saatchi tackled the briefs set by their Health Education Council client with fearless originality.

The approach had been established at Charles's consultancy, Cramer Saatchi, just before Saatchi & Saatchi was launched. Here, a brief about contraception was answered with one of the company's most famous ads. Above the headline, 'WOULD YOU BE MORE CAREFUL IF IT WAS YOU THAT GOT PREGNANT?', was a photograph of a man who appeared to be in the latter stages of pregnancy. The legendary Pregnant Man.

Originally created as a poster for use in GP surgeries, the account director, Alex Fynn, points out it was adapted in 1973 to become one of the press ads in a contraception campaign he was in charge of. The provocative directness of the Pregnant Man was applied to numerous health subjects by Saatchi & Saatchi. An ad about food hygiene described in detail the unpleasant habits flies have when they land on food, including how they vomit on it to make it softer for them to eat. The copy concluded with the alarming thought, 'And then...it's your turn'.

A press ad, as part of a test campaign for anti-alcoholism in the north-east of England, featured a photograph of a bruised child looking straight into the camera with the words, '8 PINTS OF LAGER AND 6 DOUBLE WHISKIES A NIGHT AREN'T DOING HER ANY GOOD'. An anti-smoking ad showed a close-up of someone's nicotine-stained hands using a nailbrush. The stark headline read: 'YOU CAN'T SCRUB YOUR LUNGS CLEAN'.

This is what happens when a fly lands on your food.

Flies can't eat solid food, so to soften it up they vomit on it. Then they stamp the vomit in until it's a liquid, usually stamping in a few germs for good measure. Then when it's good and runny they suck it all back again, probably dropping some excrement at the same time. And then, when they've finished eating, it's your turn.

Cover food. Cover eating and drinking utensils. Cover dustbins.

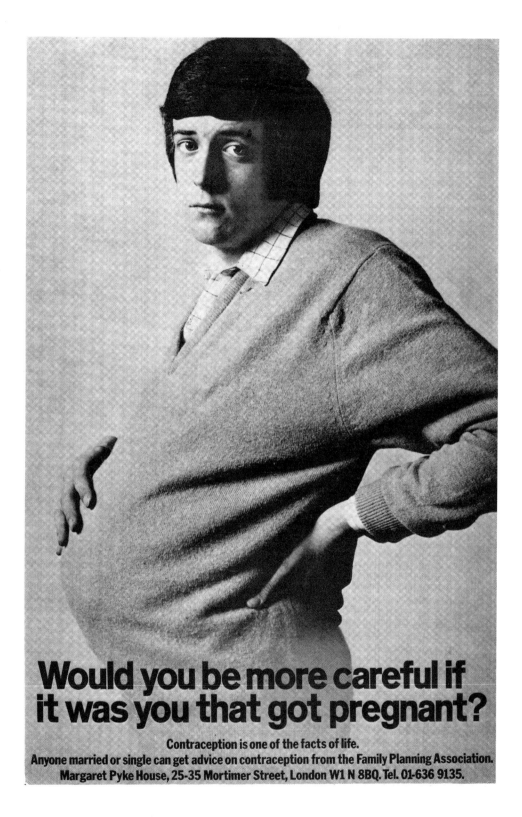

Would you be more careful if it was you that got pregnant?

Contraception is one of the facts of life.
Anyone married or single can get advice on contraception from the Family Planning Association.
Margaret Pyke House, 25-35 Mortimer Street, London W1 N 8BQ. Tel. 01-636 9135.

Social work

-273

From these beginnings, a vast body of outstanding creative work for social issues and charities has been developed over the years, and in 2000 a book, *Social Work: Saatchi & Saatchi's Cause-Related Ideas,* was produced by the publisher –273. It's near-300 pages are laden with examples of ideas from around the Saatchi & Saatchi global network, such as the highly controversial 1996 poster for the International Fund for Animal Welfare created by Saatchi & Saatchi Italy. It features the Marquise Marina Ripa di Meana, the Italian ambassador for the fund. She stands, facing the camera, completely naked, above the headline, 'THE ONLY FUR I'M NOT ASHAMED TO WEAR'. The agency's CEO, Paolo Ettorre, was briefly arrested for obscenity.

What the Pregnant Man had given birth to was a body of creative work unmatched by any other agency network. Taboos were tackled for the first time. For example, an advertisement in the UK for the NSPCC (National Society for the Prevention of Cruelty to Children) features the face of a middle-aged man with the headline: 'WHAT'S IT LIKE TO BE RAPED AS A 3 YEAR OLD? A VICTIM EXPLAINS.' The reader thinks the man is the perpetrator, but he's the victim.

Another category Saatchi & Saatchi revolutionized was political advertising. As mentioned in Chapter 1, before Saatchis began applying their creativity to the Conservative Party, political advertising largely consisted of bland and largely meaningless tub-thumping slogans. Saatchis changed all that. With the agency's help, the Conservatives came out fighting, focusing on their rivals' failings rather than on their own intentions and policies. It was a neat strategy, because it was all about the implied promise that things would be better if you voted Conservative.

Saatchis' involvement wasn't limited to the advertising. The agency also wrote and produced highly creative party political broadcasts (PPBs). For the first time, PPBs had ideas in them, rather than the dull, conventional, grey-suited talking

So many people were stopping to read this when it appeared as a crosstrack poster on London Underground, it had to be moved to a safer, less congested location further down the platform.

What's it like to be raped as a 3 year old? A victim explains.

NSPCC

4 May 1979. The day
the UK changed for ever.

heads. And for the first time, a political party was treated like a brand
– a brand that understood its potential consumers' needs. After
being in opposition for five years, the Conservative Party won the
1979 General Election, and remained in government for eighteen
years, winning the next three elections, in 1983, 1987 and 1992,
with Saatchi & Saatchi as their agency.

The company's involvement in politics wasn't limited to the UK.
In South Africa, Saatchi & Saatchi's associate agency played an
important role in the country's tumultuous changes in the 1980s and
1990s. Jurie Snyman, the agency's CEO, describes what happened:
'The South African government realized that change was inevitable
and started a process to test the water amongst the white electorate.
This was done in referenda in 1982 and 1987. We were asked to
handle all communications to promote the 'yes for change' vote and
decided to accept the job. We came in for a lot of criticism from
various groupings because this meant working for the unpopular
ruling political party. But both campaigns were highly successful
with overwhelming majorities for the yes vote.

'The last election when only whites voted was in 1989, and we
once again handled the advertising and communications for the
ruling National Party. They were re-elected with a big majority and
negotiations with black South Africans gained a lot of momentum
which resulted in the release of Nelson Mandela (early in 1990) and
free and fair elections in 1994.' The success of the South African
agency with their 'yes for change' campaigns influenced the
decision, a decade later, by the 'Yes' campaign in Northern Ireland

to enlist the help of Saatchi & Saatchi, London. The campaign was seeking a positive result in a referendum on the Good Friday Peace Agreement. The agency chairman, Alan Bishop, who led the agency's team, was described by the campaign's director, Quintin Oliver, as 'riveting'.

The campaign's chair, Paul Nolan, said, 'Alan Bishop gave us lots of priceless advice and lots of personal support, and when the Saatchi billboard design came in we knew we had produced the visual icon of the referendum.'

The 'visual icon' was made up of two road signs. One was an arrow pointing ahead, the other the sign for a dead end. When it came to the vote on both sides of the Irish border, 71 per cent voted in favour in Northern Ireland, and 94 per cent in the Republic.

But then, even by 1984 Saatchi & Saatchi's involvement in politics had developed from creating provocative election posters and PPBs, as typographer, Dave Wood reveals. At that stage, Tim Bell was in semi-exile, his relationship with Charles and Maurice having soured for a variety of reasons. However, his relationship with Margaret Thatcher was the absolute opposite. Wood says he was asked by Bell one late afternoon if he could come to his new offices, two blocks from the agency. 'Tim explained that,

'Tonight, we're going to write to every coal miner in the country'.

The miners' strike was tearing the country apart and had brought Margaret Thatcher's government head to head with the NUM (National Union of Mineworkers) president, Arthur Scargill, and violent clashes between striking miners, non-striking miners and the police had become an everyday news item. As Wood explains, 'Also present that night was a mysterious journalist by the name of David Hart who ran a right-wing organization called "Committee for a Free Britain", and apparently he had been given virtual carte blanche to deal with the strike head on.'

Wood's job was to prepare the artwork of the letter being written to the miners, ready for printing. The letter was finished by about 10 p.m., and Wood and Bell's secretary ('the fastest typist I'd ever seen', Wood says) headed for Claridge's Hotel to meet (later Sir) Ian MacGregor, the Chairman of the National Coal Board, in the luxury suite kept at the hotel by David Hart.

National Coal Board
Hobart House, Grosvenor Place, London SW1X 7AE

CHAIRMAN
Ian MacGregor

June, 1984

Dear Colleague,

<u>YOUR FUTURE IN DANGER</u>

I am taking the unusual step of writing to you at home because I want every man
and woman who has a stake in the coal industry to realise clearly the damage
which will be done if this disastrous strike goes on a long time.

The leaders of the NUM have talked of it continuing into the winter. Now that
our talks with them have broken down this is a real possibility. It could go on
until December or even longer. In which case the consequences for everybody
will be very grave.

Your President talks continually of keeping the strike going indefinitely until
he achieves "victory".

I would like to tell you, not provocatively or as a threat, why that will not
happen however long the strike lasts.

What this strike is really about is that the NUM leadership is preventing the
development of an efficient industry. We have repeatedly explained that we are
seeking to create a higher volume, lower cost industry which will be profitable,
well able to provide superior levels of earnings while still being able to
compete with foreign coal. To achieve this, huge sums of money are being
invested in new equipment; last year it was close to £800 million and we expect
to continue a similarly high rate of investment in the years ahead. Our
proposals mean, short term, cutting out some of the uneconomic pits and looking
for about 20,000 voluntary redundancies – the same as last year. The redundancy
payments are now more generous than ever before for those who decide not to take
alternative jobs offered in the industry.

However long the strike goes on I can assure you that we will end up, through
our normal consultative procedures, with about the same production plans as
those we discussed with your representatives on 6th March last.

But the second reason why continuing the strike will not bring the NUM "victory"
is this: in the end nobody will win. Everybody will lose – and lose
disastrously.

Many of you have already lost more than £2,000 in earnings and have seen your
savings disappear. If the strike goes on until December it will take many of
you years to recover financially and also more jobs may be lost – and all for
nothing.

I have been accused of planning to butcher the industry. I have no such intention or desire. I want to build up the industry into one we can all be proud to be part of.

But if we cannot return to reality and get back to work then the industry may well be butchered. But the butchers will not be the Coal Board.

You are all aware that mines which are not constantly maintained and worked deteriorate in terms of safety and workability.

AT THE PRESENT TIME THERE ARE BETWEEN 20 and 30 pits which are viable WHICH WILL BE IN DANGER OF NEVER RE-OPENING IF WE HAVE A LENGTHY STRIKE.

This is a strike which should never have happened. It is based on very serious misrepresentation and distortion of the facts. At great financial cost miners have supported the strike for fourteen weeks because your leaders have told you this .....

> That the Coal Board is out to butcher the coal industry.
> That we plan to do away with 70,000 jobs.
> That we plan to close down around 86 pits, leaving only 100 working collieries.

IF THESE THINGS WERE TRUE I WOULD NOT BLAME MINERS FOR GETTING ANGRY OR FOR BEING DEEPLY WORRIED. BUT THESE THINGS ARE ABSOLUTELY UNTRUE. I STATE THAT CATEGORICALLY AND SOLEMNLY. YOU HAVE BEEN DELIBERATELY MISLED.

The NUM, which called the strike, will end it only when you decide it should be ended.

I would like you to consider carefully, so we can get away from the tragic violence and pressures of the mass pickets, whether this strike is really in your interest.

I ask you to join your associates who have already returned to work so that we can start repairing the damage and building up a good future.

Sincerely,

Ian MacGregor

According to Wood, MacGregor was there with a member of the House of Lords. They'd been enjoying a bottle of Hart's finest malt whisky. Wood handed MacGregor a copy of the letter, which he read slowly. He looked up, said, 'Excellent,' and took another sip of malt. (Incidentally, MacGregor always called Bell 'Doctor Bell', acknowledging his role as a spin doctor.)

By 8 a.m. the next morning, 200,000 copies of the letter had been printed and a small army of envelope stuffers and labellers was waiting at the National Coal Board's offices when Wood delivered them there. The letter went out to every miner as planned. Copies were also sent to the media. And Wood says, 'A few days later the press was full of articles and comments about this controversial letter.' But he reflects that he was 'never comfortable or proud of my involvement'.

Saatchi & Saatchi were also first to create corporate advertising that imparted significant information about companies that, far from being traditionally dull and self-important, actually entertained and connected. In a similar vein to the 1975 Dunlop commercial (see Chapter 6), which was packed with impressive information as well as being visually irresistible, in 1983 British Airways briefed Saatchis to create a commercial that would give the world a clearer idea of how successful 'The World's Favourite Airline' actually was, ahead of privatization. However, at the time, the airline was losing £300 million a year and had just laid off 26,000 people. The commercial had to inspire confidence in the City of London, but it also had to inspire BA staff and sell tickets.

Campaignlive, the online version of *Campaign* magazine, summarizes the commercial, called 'Manhattan': 'The Saatchi & Saatchi ad, the first of its kind to encapsulate such diverse requirements, was based on a simple premise: that the number of people carried across the Atlantic each year by BA was greater than the population of Manhattan.' And the commercial took that fact and demonstrated it in spectacular fashion by showing a lit-up Manhattan island coming in to land at London's Heathrow Airport at night. A triumph of film-making (by Richard Loncraine). And a triumph for creative communications by the late Phil Mason and the late Rita Dempsey, art director and copywriter respectively.

'Manhattan' lands: Saatchi's relationship with BA takes off.

Over the years, Saatchi & Saatchi continued to create corporate campaigns for some of the UK's best known and biggest companies, including BP, ICI, Cadbury Schweppes, Pilkington and BT. Graham Smith, the former new business director at Saatchis, says that the agency's corporate advertising was 'a great thing for me in new business. One, the ads were very good. Two, I could chat about "changing perceptions" in a conversation, the fact that the consumer doesn't like a vacuum and will fill it with bad news rather than good.'

Saatchi & Saatchi pioneered takeover advertising too. Through its Cunard account the agency was called in by Cunard's parent company, Trafalgar House, when it launched a bid for rival shipping company P&O in 1983.

The main battle was between Trafalgar House and P&O, led by (later Sir) Nigel Broackes and Jeffrey (later Lord) Sterling respectively. But a secondary battle was joined between Saatchi & Saatchi and creative arch-rivals at the time, CDP, who were working for P&O. After Saatchis fired the first shot, both sides set about running uncompromising newspaper advertisements. This was clearly an exciting new game, and the fact that Charles Saatchi showed great interest in the work proved the point.

Richard Myers and fellow writer James Lowther found out just how interested Charles was when they returned to the agency from one of the regular early morning meetings with Trafalgar House and their various legal and financial advisors, feeling rather pleased with themselves. Charles was in Jeremy Sinclair's office, waiting for them. Debriefing him about the meeting, Lowther mentioned an idea he and Myers had had for an advertisement while they'd been with the client, who loved it. By contrast, Charles hated it and said so very clearly. (He was right about the ad, in fact.)

After the verbal roasting they got, Myers and Lowther skulked back to their offices down a long, long corridor. Almost there and some considerable distance from Sinclair's office, another writer, David Partridge, enquired in his best laconic, 'Get a bit of a wigging, did we?' Ultimately, after the bid had been referred to the Monopolies and Mergers Commission and Trafalgar House were given the go ahead, they decided not to proceed. But the new game of takeover advertising had only just begun.

'We were involved in a series of high-profile takeover battles: Guinness buying Bell's, Allied-Lyons's valiant defence against Elders XL, Argyll's scuppered attempt to take over the Distillers Company.' Patrick Hanson-Lowe, who was a Saatchi account handler at the time, credits Saatchi deputy chairman, the late John Spratling's contact with Ernest Saunders of Guinness for the agency's involvement, but adds that he 'quickly handed over to the adeptness, perspicacity and irresistible charm of Jennifer Laing'.

'In those days, Ernest was heading up Guinness Plc. He had been an ad man at JWT and a marketing man at Unilever (both then unusual backgrounds for a company CEO, by the way). This gave him the idea of using marketing and advertising in takeover bids to a much greater extent than ever before.'

Whether Saunders was inspired by the Trafalgar House versus P&O case is debatable but, as Hanson-Lowe says, Saunders liked

Saatchis fired the first shot in the great naval battle of 1983.

BELLS ON THE ROCKS?

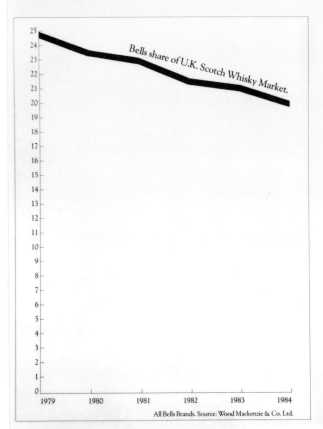

Bells share of U.K. Scotch Whisky Market.

All Bells Brands. Source: Wood Mackenzie & Co. Ltd.

Bells share of the UK Scotch Whisky market has declined by 20% since 1980.

It is no longer the number one selling Scotch Whisky in Scotland.

Alarmingly, Bells relies on the UK market for 54 per cent of total volume sales. (The average for the rest of the industry is 13 per cent.)

Overseas, Bells has repeatedly failed to make a breakthrough in the crucial US Scotch Whisky Market. Bells share of this market in 1984 was a mere 0.2 per cent.

Yet the Board of Bells has given no indication that it even recognises the problem, let alone produced plans to overcome it.

Bells is a great brand and Guinness can revitalise it. If you accept our offer, we believe your shares will be revitalised too.

GUINNESS PLC

DRAUGHT AND BOTTLED GUINNESS, HARE KALIBER, DRUMMONDS, MARTIN THE NEWSAGENT, LAVELLS, 7-ELEVEN STORES, CHAMPNEYS AND STORO CASTLE HEALTH RESORTS, NATURE'S BEST VITAMINS, GUINNESS PUBLISHING.

Guinness is good for Bells. Guinness shares are good for you.

the strategy of 'talking directly to shareholders and journalists and drumming up popular support and getting an edge on the fusty world of the opponent's bankers' use of polite announcements and tombstone ads. Now we were talking about full pages. Creative. Run of paper. In the *Sunday Times* at the front. Not just a dense quarter page in the City section of the *Daily Telegraph*.'

While it lasted, takeover advertising was perhaps the most physically and mentally demanding work one would ever experience. With a takeover battle in full swing, new ads were written and produced on a daily basis. Many of these were then rewritten during the day as the state of the battle shifted. As Hanson-Lowe says, 'In the Allied-Lyons defence, we were doing a new ad every day. Created. Shot. And repro'd. This put an enormous strain on the agency production department as they had to deliver physical (printing) plates. We solved the problem of getting them to the newspaper presses in the north of the country on time by using helicopters. And charging delivery at £40,000 a week.'

The normal deadlines and hours that agencies work simply didn't apply, but as Richard Myers remembers, 'adrenalin-fuelled, the whole thing was deeply exhilarating and satisfying'. Being present at meetings with the clients and their armies of lawyers, bankers, brokers and other advisors, he had a sense of witnessing, first-hand, corporate history being made. 'One of the most memorable aspects of the process was seeing truly momentous decisions being made in an instant, by business leaders blessed with a powerful mix of self-assurance, intellect and fearlessness.'

As Hanson-Lowe recounts, 'One night at the Guinness head office in Portman Square with Ernest Saunders and his bankers etc present, non-executive director and family member Jonathan Guinness was told politely to leave the room as they were about to discuss "bid strategy".'

Having worked on the Guinness takeover bid for Bell's, Richard Myers finds this next Hanson-Lowe recollection particularly heart-warming: 'One night, one of our Guinness printing plates was late getting to the *Perthshire Advertiser*, in Bell's home town. The driver's lights were failing. The police stopped him. When he explained what he was delivering they showed their support for the takeover and gave him an escort all the way.'

Every takeover the agency worked on ramped up the volume, intensity, vitriol and effect of the ads. There was a lot of resistance from the bankers and lawyers, who favoured secrecy and back room deals. As it turned out, this was just a little too much when Saunders, Jack Lyons, Anthony Parnes and Gerald Ronson were charged and convicted of offences relating to the Guinness takeover of Distillers. Two years later, the takeover advertising game was over when display advertising was banned. An attempt to control the content of the advertising through the regulatory Takeover Panel had failed.

In addition to being first in creating or revolutionizing advertising categories, Saatchi & Saatchi can also claim a significant number of media, creative and production firsts.

Ignoring the mildly cynical, yet solid principal that if anything can go wrong, it will, in 1975 Saatchi & Saatchi came up with an idea for their *London Evening News* client: live TV commercials. The soundness of the strategy – to demonstrate the immediacy of the paper's news coverage – was beyond question, but it threw up a whole bag full of technical and bureaucratic issues. Top of the challenges was how the ITCA (Independent Television Companies Association) would be able to deal with this pioneering proposition; the process wasn't exactly engineered to cope with anything remotely live.

A typical film can of the time. Approximately 28 cm (11 inches) in diameter.

The ITCA Copy Submission Requirements (1974)

Speedy Copy Clearance.
We want to help you by clearing copy and approving commercials without delay. Because of our statutory responsibilities there are certain procedures which we must follow. Please help us to help you by complying with these notes: we have made them as simple and straightforward as possible.

Scripts.
As soon as a pre-production script is available, 10 copies should be submitted to ITCA, addressed to:
Copy Department,
Independent Television Companies Association
52-66 Mortimer Street, LONDON W1 N 8AN.

At ITCA we deal with many thousands of scripts each year and a degree of standardisation in script information and layout has been found to be most helpful. The following format indicates the ideal and has been adopted, with slight variations, by the majority of advertising agencies:

- Agency's name, address and telephone number
- Date of script
- Production date
- Name of advertiser
- Name of product
- Transmission date(s)
- Transmission area(s)
- Reference number, title and length of commercial
- Name(s) of artist(s)
- Name of agency executive responsible for ITCA negotiations
- Whether film, VTR, or cassette
- Colour or Monochrome

FRAME	VISION	SOUND
1........................		
2........................		
3........................		
Etc.		

Frames should always be numbered, as this aids quick reference to a particular section of the script in any discussions and subsequent ITCA comment. When a production company submits a script, the name of the advertising agency concerned should also be included on the script.

The great majority of scripts submitted to us present no major problem and are normally cleared within a few days. We will contact you immediately by telephone if there are any problems so that they may be speedily resolved. One copy of the script is then returned, together with a form confirming ITCA approval and any agreed amendments, and indicating any points requiring particular care in production.

Storyboards.
Although a script is normally sufficient for copy clearance purposes, a story board is often desirable and sometimes essential in cases where a script alone cannot adequately describe a visual sequence, which might give rise to a misleading impression, or offend against acceptable good taste or decency. In such cases 10 copies of a storyboard should be submitted so that the visual treatment may be fully understood and considered. A separate script is then unnecessary, provided the storyboard carries all the other information and detail normally shown on a script.

Evidence.
Factual claims of any description in a script cannot be approved without full supporting evidence. For example, it is essential that where new claims are based on clinical, scientific or technical tests or reports, a copy of this evidence should accompany the script so that it may be submitted immediately to ITCA's medical or technical advisers. Similarly, evidence in connection with sales claims, competition details, guarantee cards, product formulae, special offers, etc. should normally be provided for examination at the same time as the script.

Films.
One print of every new commercial must be submitted to ITCA for approval before transmission and it is advisable for this to be done before bulk prints are ordered in case any change should be required. Films should be delivered to:

Copy Department,
Independent Television Companies Association,
52-66 Mortimer Street,
LONDON W1N 8AN.

All films must be delivered in separate 200ft. cans, clearly labelled with:

(a) the name of the agency, advertiser and product
(b) the identification number and title of the film (which must also be clearly marked on the film itself)
(c) the duration of the film
(d) the word 'Colour' if the film is in colour

Every film must be accompanied by:

(a) three copies of the post-production script, which must accurately represent the finished commercial and carry the identification number and title of the film
(b) three copies of a consignment note (plus a fourth copy if one is required as a receipt) setting out :
   1. name and address of the agency
   2. name of the advertiser
   3. name of the product
   4. identification number, title and length of the film
   5. transmission area(s)
   6. transmission date(s)
   7. name(s) of the artist(s) - indicating sound or vision
   8. full music details for copyright purposes
(c) an addressed label for the return of the film (unless the address is already clearly printed on the film-can).

Approved films are returned accompanied by one stamped copy of the post production script and an ITCA form confirming approval. If approval is subject to any special conditions, the form will indicate these.

At the same time, one copy of the consignment note is sent to the Performing Right Society and one to the Mechanical Copyright Protection Society. There after individual Programme Companies notify the two Societies of every transmission of the commercial. (Initial copyright clearance must, of course, be arranged by the advertiser or agency.)

In the event of a commercial not being acceptable the advertising agency or advertiser will be contacted immediately by telephone. It must be emphasised that ITCA approval of a commercial is in terms of copy only; it does not mean that the technical quality of the commercial will necessarily be accepted by the Programme Companies as suitable for trans mission, either in monochrome or colour.

Double-Heads.

Where there is any doubt about a particular visual sequence it is advisable, in order to avoid unnecessary expense and trouble, for a double-head version of the film to be submitted for preliminary viewing and advice, before a married print is made. For double-heads :

(a) full academy leaders on both sound and visual tracks are required
(b) leaders should be marked for synchronisation
(c) synchronisation marks should not be placed on any white spacing between the film and the leader
(d) care should be taken to ensure that leaders are joined to magnetic double-heads so that the sound tracks are in line with each other
(e) three copies of the post-production script should accompany every double-head
(f) advertising agencies should make arrangements for double-heads to be collected after viewing at ITCA

A married print must still be submitted in the usual way for final approval when completed, at which stage the full documentation listed under 'Films' above will be required.

VTRs and Cassettes.

With the exception of local commercials (to be shown in one area only) which may be cleared by the Programme Company concerned, requirements for VTR and Cassette commercials are basically the same as for films above, a half-inch Sony Videotape or Philips Cassette taking the place of the film print.

Immediate viewing for clearance purposes can be arranged whenever necessary in order not to lose the advantage of speed offered by VTR and Cassette. Advance arrangements should normally be made if clearance is required outside business hours.

And this is how the clearance process was described at the time:

'With a busy traffic department to ensure efficient and speedy control of workflow, the main task of scrutinising scripts and films is carried out by four separate Copy Groups. The head of each of these copy groups is responsible for one-quarter of the scripts and films that come to ITCA. While there will be some regular interchange, each group will service the same agencies for some time so the Group Heads and Executives will get to know their opposite numbers in the agencies concerned and become familiar with the products which the agencies handle and the problems about them which have already arisen and been solved. There is a great reliance on personal contact, much of the work being done between the Copy Group and the agencies on the telephone. Each morning the Head of Copy Clearance with his Deputy holds a meeting with the four Copy Group Heads. The object of this is to seek a joint Secretariat solution to any difficult or border-line case, subject to consultation and agreement with the IBA, and to decide whether any matter needs to be referred to the Copy Committee. By doing this, the Secretariat can keep a consistent standard of interpretation of the Code. The Head of Copy Clearance with his Deputy are responsible for the administration of the system and for its efficiency. They are always ready with the Group Head concerned to meet agency or advertiser representatives to solve problems.'

Fortunately, David Slade, the Copy Group Head allocated to Saatchi & Saatchi could not have been more helpful and less bureaucratic. Creative director at the time, Jeremy Sinclair, readily acknowledges Slade's collaboration in making it possible for this improbable campaign to see the light of day.

Ron Leagas recalls another first on TV in the UK. 'Carmen heated curlers bought into a media plan, unused until then, to make a small budget seem big on regional TV (heavily southern biased where the big retail buyers lived).

It used seven second ads, topping and tailing ad breaks with a simple but clever and inexpensive film showing, in the first spot, a close-up of a roller in hair, and in the last, the roller being taken out with a curl bouncing up and down like a spring. Several different voice-overs were used with the same two films.'

Yet another TV first is remembered by Alex Fynn. The commercial Saatchi & Saatchi created for Tottenham Hotspur (Spurs) was the first ever for a football team. 'The brief', he says, 'was to increase attendances at matches.' The commercial showed the Spurs team running out onto the pitch announced by the voice-over, 'Here comes the Spurs team, led out by Ossie Ardiles, Ray Clemence...followed by Mrs Riddlington, the Jones family, Peter

Cook [the comedian]…' The final line was, 'This Saturday, Spurs will be fielding 35,000 against Coventry. Make sure you're one of the team.' (Incidentally, Fynn is well known in the UK as a soccer pundit and has written a number of books on the subject.)

Away from television, in 1984, when Allen Chevalier was vice president, managing director of Saatchis in Paris, the agency created the first ever musical magazine ad. The client was IBM. Chevalier received a letter that read: 'The IBM-PC insert is astonishing. As you know I now have one hundred copies in my office, which I hand to everyone I meet with great pride. You must all be thrilled by the reaction to it – I know I am to be associated with it. With many congratulations. Sincerely, Maurice Saatchi.'

There's an impressive list of firsts for Saatchi & Saatchi, in fact. British Airways 'Face' was the first commercial to cost £1 million to make. Saatchi & Saatchi Denmark created the first all-metal poster, for Audi, that rusted over time. Copywriter Peers Carter and art director Matt Ryan at Saatchi & Saatchi London created a poster for the Motor Neurone Disease Association, featuring a patient photographed by James Cotier. The poster was the first designed to fade, which it did over three weeks, once the necessary ink formula had been discovered by Bob Holt, the agency's production director. (Poignantly, the patient featured in the poster died of the disease during the three weeks.)

According to Holt, Saatchis also pioneered the use of a four-colour printing machine for posters. Critical to Saatchi & Saatchi's success with their famous Silk Cut poster campaign was the accurate reproduction of the colour purple, which,

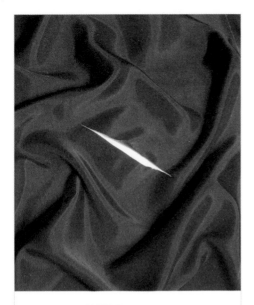

LOW TAR As defined by H.M. Government
DANGER: Government Health WARNING:
CIGARETTES CAN SERIOUSLY DAMAGE YOUR HEALTH

A Silk Cut ad, before the ban on cigarette advertising, from the Saatchi & Saatchi archives.

unbelievably, was not possible until Holt turned his garage at home into a printing ink laboratory and solved the problem. He recalls too that Saatchis used the world's first ad van with the message, 'TAKE WEDNESDAY OFF AND GIVE THE JAPANESE ECONOMY A BOOST'. The ad was for Conservative Central Office and it clearly upset someone because, parked outside the Labour Party's headquarters, one of the van's tyres was slashed.

As well as making pioneering steps forward in print advertising, Saatchis were also streets ahead in finding new ways to sell. New York became home to the first spectacular 'living billboard' for Delta Air Lines in Times Square, in the summer of 1997. The agency had built a life-size cutaway fuselage of a Delta jet, with the seats occupied by real people and real flight attendants serving them. This innovation was designated by *Mediaweek* magazine as the Best Use of Out-Of-Home in its annual 'Media Plan of the Year' competition. And for its creativity, the 'living billboard' was judged to be the best of all ads in the outdoor category over the previous year.

A big, new outdoor advertising idea lands in New York's Times Square.

Saatchis London can claim another first, again for an airline. Copywriter John Pallant describes how he and his creative partner came up with the idea: 'Art director Matt Ryan and I were working on a brief for British Airways "Short Breaks", promoting deals on flights for romantic weekends away in the spring in European cities. The brief was simply "Dirty Weekends", so it was quite fun to work on. We had been asked to come up with a poster campaign, which we did, but we also had an idea for a cinema commercial for which, at that point, there was no budget.

'Over lunch one day, we explained the idea to our creative director, Paul Arden. Paul was a passionate person, known for his childlike enthusiasm for ideas (as well as his tantrums), and he got so excited about this one, he immediately jumped up and abandoned the lunch halfway through, insisting that we all go back to the office to tell managing director David Kershaw about it. The idea was this: the commercial (called "Surprise, Surprise") would begin on the cinema screen with a young man and woman walking arm in arm through various romantic scenes of Paris, while the voice-over said, "Why not surprise your loved one with a British Airways Short Break..." At this point, an actress planted in the cinema audience would pretend to recognize the man as her boyfriend, cheating on her with this other woman in the film on the screen, and start to get annoyed. Standing up, she would start to yell at the screen to attract his attention. And surprisingly, the man on the screen would appear to be able to see the woman in the audience and engage her in an awkward conversation in which he would try to explain himself to both her, and of course, also to the girl he was in Paris with. Having none of it, the woman in the audience would dump him, and storm out of the cinema. And the other woman on the screen would also dump him and storm off, leaving him on his own in a park in Paris. The voice-over, which had stopped for the duration of this "embarrassing" interruption, would then hastily wrap things up, and the commercial would end.

'Well, everyone was excited about the idea, and it was shown to the team at British Airways. They liked it, too, and said they wanted to make it happen. But the weeks started to go by, and there was still no sign of the extra budget from them to make that possible. So the Saatchi management decided to pay for the production of

Lord King.
'Mrs Thatcher's favourite businessman'.

the idea themselves, and to take it to Lord King, the BA Chairman, to get the go-ahead. With our producer Mark Hanrahan, we approached a friend of ours, Frank Budgen, who had previously worked as a copywriter at Saatchi, and had just started directing. As this would be a good way to showcase his talent, his production company, The Paul Weiland Film Company, kindly offered to produce the film for us, without their usual mark up.

'There was a slight hiccup when Paul Arden had one of his tantrums and rejected our casting for the characters. He had imagined them as a very stylish, elegant, good-looking couple, whereas we saw them as more ordinary, everyday people. We took a risk, and decided to ignore our creative director's direction and went ahead and did it our way, because we thought it would be funnier.

'Finally, when the film was ready, Lord King and his marketing team were invited to the agency, where we had our own little preview cinema, to see it. We had cast an experienced stand-up comedienne as the woman who would sit in the audience and cause the disturbance. It all worked perfectly.

'Lord King was delighted and asked if it would be possible to recreate this little piece of theatre at some of his dinner parties at home. He left telling his marketing people to make it happen. And so it did. British Airways paid for the production and for our actress, Jenny, to go on tour with the commercial all over the UK. And she came back with some funny stories of her experience, one about a cinema where some staff had not been informed of her appearance and tried to eject her, midway through her performance.

'The commercial got a huge amount of free media coverage, possibly more than any other Saatchi commercial at that time, and won awards at all the festivals it was entered in. And Paul Arden agreed that it had been a good decision to ignore him on this occasion.'

Matt Ryan recalls the possible inspiration for 'Surprise, Surprise': 'In New York on some down-time after a shoot, John and

I went to the cinema to see the newly opened *Untouchables*. We thought it was hilarious how the cinema audience shouted at the screen, as if able to affect the action: "He's behind you muthafucker, he's gotta piece!!"'

Account director Paul Burns describes a rather different and very unlikely creative first. 'For our Jammie Dodger biscuit client, we had created the JDWWJWF (the Jammie Dodger World Wide Jam Wrestling Federation, of course). The campaign involved the creation of a load of surreal Jam Wrestling characters, similar to the strange wrestlers kids loved in WWWF. Someone suggested that one of the characters, the Ginger Crab, should stand in the 2001 parliamentary general election for London's Kensington and Chelsea seat against Michael Portillo [the well-known Conservative politician who had lost his Enfield Southgate seat in the 1997 election]. A student on work placement at the Jammie Dodger's PR agency had to change his name by deed poll to Ginger Crab, so he could stand in the election representing the Jam Wrestling Party.'

A slight departure from Saatchis' usual involvement in politics.

Burns says one of his best memories was 'watching our Ginger Crab appearing on the election night TV programme, watching the count and the Ginger Crab shaking hands (claws) with Michael Portillo, as the returning officer read out the results and said, "Crab, Ginger, 100 votes".'

Politicized wrestling crabs may be quirky, but a slightly more subtle and extremely effective form of attention-getting came when Saatchi & Saatchi London were first to use a flash mob in a commercial, for their T-Mobile client. The campaign line the idea emerged from was 'LIFE IS FOR SHARING'. On a cold January morning, as commuters poured off their trains into London's Liverpool Street station, the huge main area of the terminus was filled with music. A few people, dressed like regular commuters, started to dance. More and more joined in until there were 350 dancers, all doing their moves.

How to get advertising to make the news.

The flash mob did exactly what it was designed to do. It got countless commuters to take out their phones and share what they were witnessing with calls, texts, photos and videos. Many of them joined in for an unusual dancing start to their working day. The event was filmed and a commercial, edited from the coverage, was on air within thirty-six hours. Account director James Griffiths has pointed out that as well as featuring on 70,000 blogs, 'Dance' has gone on to have, so far, well over 40 million views on YouTube, and has inspired sixty-eight separate Facebook groups.

Saatchi & Saatchi have always been successful at persuading people with no previous advertising appearances or involvement to their (famous) names, to change their minds. As well as Cat Stevens finally allowing his music to be used for New Zealand Telecom (see Chapter 6), in the UK, the theoretical physicist Stephen Hawking agreed to appear in a commercial for the first time, in a beautifully emotional commercial for British Telecom.

Peter Gibb's 'Mud Men' shoot in Papua New Guinea for Silk Cut cigarettes was the first ever advertising commission taken on by photographer Sebastião Salgado (see Chapter 6). A commercial for Panasonic is recalled by Pete Watkins, mainly for its soundtrack. 'All You Need Is Love' was the first time a Beatles track (and in its original form too) had ever been used in a commercial. Similarly, Roger Waters of Pink Floyd was persuaded to allow his 'Is There Anybody Out There?' to be the soundtrack for a powerful Samaritans commercial.

Saatchi & Saatchi have also been instrumental over the years in changing the way advertising goes about its business. John Honsinger set up the Sales Promotion Agency in 1980 to handle through-the-line advertising in which mass advertising is used to form a consumer database that can then be used for direct marketing activities. Honsinger recalls: 'SPA was notable for two things – it was the first home-grown subsidiary of Saatchis (all others being acquisitions), and it was the first fully integrated above and below the line agency.' While Charles Fallon recalls how, when he founded Saatchi Interactive in 1994, it was almost certainly the first digital agency in London.

Team Saatchi interior 'decorated' by graffiti artist Temper.

In the same year, Mike Parker created and launched Team Saatchi. This was a visionary innovation. The concept sprang from Parker's belief that small-budget accounts could be serviced profitably, but not in the business environment of the main Saatchi & Saatchi agency. Parker, an Olympic hurdler in his younger days, is one of the most fearless and persuasive people Richard Myers ever had the pleasure of working with. In Team Saatchi he established a

One of Temper's ceiling tiles from Team Saatchi.

'non-hierarchical, informal, graffiti-clad, open environment, where the client was "placed" at the centre of his or her team and encouraged to shape it to suit their way of working'.

Parker set about using his considerable selling skills and impressive network of contacts to keep a stream of new business opportunities coming into Team Saatchi. Accounts or projects have included the BBC, Plymouth Gin, Cobra Beer, the French multinational corporation Saint-Gobain, Domino's Pizza, Sport England, DEFRA and *Closer* magazine.

Zenith Media is an outstanding example of Saatchi pioneering and one of the ways the agency has fundamentally changed the game and the landscape.

The architect of Zenith was John Perriss, the agency's media director at the time. In his proposal to his management (4 August 1987), Perriss describes the background. 'In nearly all markets in the world, advertisers are facing advertising costs inflating much faster than the general rate of inflation. There have been pauses (US networks 1986-7) but generally all advertisers have been wrestling fairly ineffectually with this. We at least can deliver a competitive result for them in this market.

'The globalization of media owners (i.e. Murdoch from the UK, US and Australia, Maxwell from the UK, Berlusconi in Southern Europe, Bertelsmann Corp. from Germany, Nihon Keizai from Japan, etc) is also adding to their power base, and intensifying advertisers' needs to have deep resources to cope with and manage these changes.'

Just thirteen months later, in the 9 September 1988 edition of *Campaign*, under an enormous front page headline,

'ZENITH: THE FACTS'.

It said, '[Zenith is] designed to combat the growing power of media owners and the world domination of a handful of media conglomerates.' Saatchi went so far as to say,

'We will be operating on level terms with the new media moguls.'

The impact of Zenith was immediate. One independent media rival, Chris Ingram, said, 'Zenith came straight into the market as a 600lb gorilla. A lot of people wanted them to fail, but they proved them all wrong.'

According to a source who prefers to remain anonymous, 'Zenith was the first to consolidate the media businesses of conventional ad agencies into a most powerful media machine – another stake in the heart of the full service agency (the first being the end of commission) – a good thing too for clients.' The same source says that non-Saatchi clients bought into the idea 'in a flash. The only delay was the resistance and rear guard of the agency establishment. It's a no-brainer from an efficiency and effectiveness standpoint. Of course, it exposed the full service agency model and what it did for its 15 per cent (less 2 per cent media).' The appeal of Zenith was irresistible because its benefits were undisputable: 'Cost and effectiveness due to economies of scale, increased effectiveness through better research, single-minded focus on media, and negotiating clout.'

It's probably true to say that Zenith launched a media revolution. In his proposal, Perriss had said, 'We live in an industry of hyperbole. But at the end of the day, we are what we do, not what we say.' In many ways this neatly summarizes Saatchi & Saatchi's willingness to seize opportunities and to be pioneers.

While Saatchi & Saatchi's spirit of opportunism continued unabated, it wasn't always shared by their clients. When the demolition of the Berlin Wall began in 1989, the agency proposed a bold idea to their Akzo paints client. Group account director Paul Cowan describes what happened: 'In mid-December 1989 we took our Akzo client out for a Christmas dinner, somewhere in the country to the west of London. We had been working on their Sandtex exterior paint brand. The brief focused on the long-lasting nature of the product.

'At the dinner, the conversation turned to the news from Berlin, and I proposed we develop a strong poster idea for Sandtex based on the thought that the product "lasts longer than the Berlin Wall" – and for it to be actually pasted on the Wall. The senior client responded very negatively to the idea. In the end I said if they did not want to use the opportunity then we would.

'The idea kept me awake that night and the following morning

I walked into (executive creative director) Paul Arden's office and asked for his support to turn the idea into a finished poster. He agreed. We came up with the line, "SAATCHI & SAATCHI. FIRST OVER THE WALL", and got the artwork prepared.'

Arden asked Cowan about the money and Cowan said he had a "fund" hidden internally for production and would use that. With (managing director) Paul Bainsfair's approval to go ahead, Cowan approached the media team, led by Charlie Makin. 'The team introduced me to a poster contractor, Primesite, who were happy to be involved on the basis that we really wouldn't know how much it would cost to bribe the guards and get a truck with contractors safely to the other side of the Berlin Wall. And back.'

Opportunism plus faith in an idea equals a world first.

Cowan believes Primesite charged around £5,000. An image of the poster with its Saatchi & Saatchi message went around the world, instantly generating huge coverage. Cowan says, 'I never bothered to ask the Akzo client if he regretted not taking up my idea.'

Saatchi & Saatchi injected creativity into their annual company reports, which makes complete sense for a creative company, of course. They produced the first 'pop-up' annual report, in which photographs of the directors stood up when the report was opened. Another Saatchi & Saatchi annual report was the first to feature a voice chip. When the report was opened, a message from worldwide CEO Kevin Roberts was heard.

What might have been.

The most notorious Saatchi & Saatchi first that didn't go quite as planned was the proposal to buy the Midland Bank – then one of the UK's four high-street clearing banks. At the time, Saatchi & Saatchi had become so much more than just an advertising agency. It had developed to a point where it accurately fitted the description of 'multi-service company'. But one key service offering was missing from their portfolio. Financial. Typically, their approach to filling this gap was not modest. They decided they wanted to own a bank.

Despite the apparent, albeit ambitious, strategic logic, the general view persists that this was simply a spectacular five vehicle collision involving chutzpah, hubris, megalomania, nemesis and naivety. And certainly, in true British style, there was a rush to climb aboard the schadenfreude express when the project came to grief. But what was the view of people working at Saatchis at the time?

From Richard Myers's point of view, the idea seemed both surreal and magnificent, almost a natural progression for the company, and a reinforcement of the company's boundless daring. But he acknowledges that his is a foot soldier's view. A senior executive at the time has a different take on it. 'Megalomania with a hint of strategy and no serious thought about how it would be managed. In other words, just like the majority of other companies bought by Saatchis at the time. It failed because it was a daft idea and there was no follow though. It was an insight into the stupidity of the holding company and its directors dominated by the brothers and most particularly Maurice, who was the driving force in this part of the business. If any lesson was learned from the Midland bid [sic], it was what not to do.'

Another senior executive, however, sees it differently. Alban Lloyd says,

'I always thought this could have been a goer, and was a great example of Saatchis' creative forward thinking when you see what happened to banks later'.

Lord (Michael) Dobbs greets a political acquaintance in parliament.

Deputy chairman, Michael (now Lord) Dobbs (and bestselling author) had a ringside seat, having worked on the argument they would pitch to the financial services sector.

He observes that, 'The City was never convinced that an advertising agency had anything to bring to retail, let alone wholesale banking. The City resented "advertising Johnnies" suggesting they knew better about the banking world's business and threatening to invade their club…We were never able to convince them that we had a robust business plan. The City concluded it was Saatchi & Saatchi that "didn't get it".'

Another possible explanation for the failure was revealed by Tim (Lord) Bell during a conversation with Simon Goode and Richard Myers. By the time of the Midland Bank episode, Bell had left Saatchi & Saatchi and his relationship with Charles and Maurice was far from friendly. His relationship with Margaret Thatcher, however, was very good. Being aware of the way the Saatchis were behaving towards Bell, she offered to help. Bell said, 'Thank you, but I'm a big boy, I can look after myself.' To which Thatcher replied, 'Even big boys need a little help from time to time.' And then, according to Bell, someone leant on Sir Kit McMahon, the chairman of Midland Bank, telling him he was not to get involved with the Saatchis. No actual bid was ever made to buy the Midland Bank, but the episode was certainly a setback. Michael Dobbs adds,

'It brought to an end the period of explosive expansion…The City made us pay a very high price for our overstretched ambitions.'

Despite its failure, this remarkable plan is an illustration of the essence of pioneering: an irresistible urge to be the first to do something, coupled with a refusal to be deterred by the inherent risk of failure.

The front cover of the 1987 Annual Report, proudly displaying the extent of the company's diversification.

Advertising
Design
Direct Marketing
Sales Promotion
Public Relations
Market Research
Corporate Identity
Display and Merchandising
Conference Management
Media Buying and Analysis
Recruitment
Management Consulting
Human Resources
Distribution Logistics
Information Systems
Remuneration and Pensions
Litigation Counselling
~~Banking~~

Chapter 6

'...AND THEN THE CAT KISSES THE MOUSE...'

You might be forgiven for thinking that
Saatchi & Saatchi's chutzpah lacked substance
and simply revolved around fame and illusion.
But the company was built on very solid foundations,
particularly with regard to its creative output.

AT THE OUTSET, Saatchi & Saatchi was blessed in having two incredible creative minds directing the work: Charles Saatchi and Jeremy Sinclair. Their near faultless and always decisive, creative judgement was matched by the smartest strategic thinking. And beyond these two invaluable attributes, they possessed an overarching ambition for the agency to be responsible for the most original advertising the public was ever likely to see.

When it came to assessing creative ideas presented to him by his department's teams of copywriters and art directors, Sinclair was a very astute psychologist. If an idea wasn't wrong, but at the same time didn't excite him, he would simply say, 'You could do that,' with the gentlest emphasis on 'could'. To a copywriter's or art director's ears this was just about the most damning comment imaginable, because it meant your idea was ordinary. In a similar vein, his critique might be, 'Well, it won't do any noticeable damage to the brand.' A creative team's response to either critique would be an overwhelming urge to leave Sinclair's office immediately and start all over again. Personal pride could mean another late night.

If Sinclair thought an idea was wrong, he would say so, and why, in a very calm, understated way. By contrast, if Charles saw an idea he thought was wrong his response could be very forthright and loud. His displeasure, however, was always short-lived, his anger faded quickly and the whole thing was soon forgotten. Sinclair, who, according to Sean O'Connor, 'has a chateau-bottled genius', was the master of self-control. Sinclair practised meditation, which probably helped.

Sinclair's coolness is typified by a story about the fabulously maverick and eccentric director Tony Kaye. Somehow, when Kaye was launching himself as a commercials director, he managed to get onto the agency's roof. From there he started throwing flyers, announcing he was the greatest British director since Alfred Hitchcock. The agency's administration director, David Forrester, was understandably alarmed about this. At the time, because of its relationship with the Conservative Party, the agency was considered a potential terrorist target. Forrester went to Sinclair's office to report what was happening. Sinclair's response was to ask, 'Is his [show] reel any good?'

Unsurprisingly then, even if Sinclair thought an idea was brilliant, his enthusiasm for it would generally extend no further than a semi-mumbled, 'Good.' This would be followed by some deeply probing questions about how the creative team thought their idea might possibly be brought to life.

Over time, this pursuit of originality instilled an attitude that became a cornerstone of the whole agency. As the agency successfully brought to life more and more extraordinary ideas, the belief was born that there wasn't anything the agency couldn't do.

For a creative, the thought was utterly liberating. And it inspired the rest of the agency never to see problems, only challenges and opportunities to shine. No one wanted to fail, particularly on a mission impossible. Anyone who didn't really care too much about failing usually ended up doing so at another agency. The belief began to be expressed as 'nothing is impossible'. The words would later be carved in stone on the top step up to the agency's reception from Charlotte Street, a move suggested by Hamish Pringle when he was vice chairman and director of marketing.

The company motto, carved into the stone front doorstep at 80 Charlotte Street.

The attitude enshrined in 'nothing is impossible' not only inspired extraordinary achievements in London, but it also travelled well (and intact) to many of the offices in the Saatchi & Saatchi global network. One of the most prodigious walkers of the walk was the sadly missed CEO of Saatchi & Saatchi Italy, Paolo Ettorre. A lawyer by training, Ettorre had the most outstanding people skills and the most impressive network of contacts to go with them. The Vatican, the Italian government and any number of Italian industrialists and the owners of world-famous luxury brands were all in Ettorre's address book. For example, private, after-hours tours of the Sistine Chapel were enjoyed by many visiting Saatchi people, by out-of-town clients and by anyone else Paolo thought might appreciate this unique privilege. He even managed to arrange a private viewing of Leonardo da Vinci's 'Last Supper' in the Convent of Santa Maria delle Grazie for the members of Saatchis' Worldwide Creative Board when the board met in Milan. But it wasn't just a private viewing.

The mural had just been restored and it hadn't even been reopened to the public yet.

But there was so much more to Ettorre than a bulgingly impressive address book. His powers of persuasion were phenomenal. In 1991, Ettore managed to get the legendary, but very reluctant Italian film director Federico Fellini to direct a series of TV commercials for Saatchi Italy's client Banca Di Roma. He then convinced the client to go with the unheard of three-minute long commercials that emerged from the shoot. As an encore, in 1993 he talked Woody Allen into directing a campaign of TV commercials for the Italian retail chain Coop.

Federico Fellini (left) with Paolo Ettorre (right).

Paolo never missed an opportunity to tackle the impossible. His office in Rome overlooked the Piazza Di Popolo, and during the summer of 1998, the perimeter of the Piazza was fenced off for restoration work. Annette Ettorre, Paolo's widow, explains how a unique opportunity was milked.

'Saatchi & Saatchi had been asked to produce a campaign to promote Puccini's opera, *Tosca*, that was to be staged in Rome's Olympic Stadium. As well as a campaign portraying opera as popular entertainment by depicting opera lovers acting like football fans, waving flags emblazoned with 'Support Puccini' and '100% Tosca' slogans, Paolo thought of utilizing the whole fence for a poster telling the story of *Tosca*. The poster was unveiled by the mayor of Rome and was listed in the Guinness Book of Records as the world's longest poster [274 by 2 metres].'

Without doubt, Ettorre knew how to create impact and how to maximize the media coverage that could go with it. In 1995 a soccer fan was killed during an Italian Serie A (championship) match. As a consequence, the Federazione Italiana Giuoco Calcio (the Italian Soccer Federation) briefed Saatchi & Saatchi to develop a campaign against violence in soccer stadia. Not for the first time, in addition to a traditional campaign, Paolo persuaded the client to do something that had never been done before. Something unthinkable, in fact.

As one might expect, rivalry between Serie A teams and their supporters is intense and, in some cases, bitter, but when the players came out for the start of all the matches in Serie A on a particular weekend they were wearing the opposing team's shirts. After reading aloud a message condemning violence, the players swapped shirts again for the kick-off. More than 1.8 billion people around the world saw this event, and the story was front-page news in every Italian paper.

On the other side of the world, Saatchi & Saatchi New Zealand demonstrated a similar commitment to achieving the presumed impossible. In the late 1990s the agency's client NZ Telecom wanted to take a step back from the retail and pricing wars waging between phone companies, and build value back into the importance of a phone call. This is how Kim Thorp, the agency's then executive creative director, recalls the campaign:

'I wrote two quite emotional scenarios. One was about the simple power of talking between two young boys from unidentified countries at war. The second was observing a young man's relationship with his father over the years until his father is no longer there. The concepts were really created with two Cat Stevens tracks in mind.'

The agency needed Cat Stevens's 'Where do the Children Play?' and 'Father and Son', but he had never allowed any of his songs to be used in advertising. It didn't look difficult, it looked impossible.

The agency TV producer Juliet Dreaver started seeking permission. Many requests over weeks and months were rejected. But then, on one of the many 'no' faxes that came back, she noticed someone had inadvertently included Cat Stevens's personal fax number. Kim Thorp wrote yet another letter which was sent, together with the scripts, to Cat Stevens's agents. And 'by mistake' to Cat Stevens's personal fax number. Thorp says, 'Again time went by and finally, almost a year to the day we started our requests, Juliet came into my room and silently handed me a sheet of paper. It was a fax of my original letter with a simple "Yes" and a signature on it from Cat Stevens.'

...and then the cat kisses the mouse.

Where dogged persistence, coupled with a little bit of luck, was the key to success with Cat Stevens, another cat story illustrates the value of blind faith in achieving the impossible. A script for a live-action TV commercial for the Solid Fuel Advisory Council in the UK called for a dog sitting in front of a coal fire to be joined by a cat. The dog and the cat kiss. They're then joined by a mouse. The cat kisses the mouse. Simple. The cosiness of a real fire unites deadly enemies. The script, written by creative team Charles Hendley, copywriter, and Adrian Kemsley, art director, was approved by the client. But then several directors took one look at the script and decided they were busy somewhere – just anywhere – else. The agency approached Tony Kaye who, fortunately, tended to focus on the end result way ahead of any difficulties that might be encountered in getting there. Today, executing the script would be simplicity itself because of developments such as CGI. But not in 1988. They had to film it 'live' and simply hope that, with three natural enemies in such close proximity, nature didn't take its course. Miraculously it didn't, and 'Furry Friends', as the commercial was called, was a huge success. Amongst other things, it was voted the most popular TV commercial in a public poll.

A few years later, Tony Kaye himself tested the 'nothing is impossible' attitude of head of TV Mark Hanrahan. Kaye was due to appear in person at the Saatchi & Saatchi New Directors' Showcase at the Cannes International Advertising Festival. His role was well-defined – he would be carried through the auditorium and on to the stage in a closed coffin, before stepping out of the coffin to the shock of the audience. But Kaye kept working on what he would do after emerging from the coffin. Hanrahan was Kaye's 'minder'.

At about 3 a.m., the night before the Showcase, Hanrahan's hotel phone rang. It was Kaye. 'I need three flamenco guitarists by eight o'clock,' he said, and rang off. Hanrahan immediately called the hotel's concierge. Within an hour the concierge called back. 'Monsieur 'ana-'aran. I am desolé. I can only provide *two* flamenco guitarists by eight o'clock. I am so very, very sorry.' Hanrahan called Kaye with this almost good news, but Kaye had changed his mind. He didn't want any flamenco guitarists now. Instead, his new idea was to emerge from the coffin with a Discman and headphones and subject the audience to a not entirely tuneful rendition of Abba's 'I Have a Dream' – unaccompanied, of course, as far as the audience was concerned.

'Furry Friends' wasn't the first time Saatchis had not allowed current technical limitations to stand in the way of a good idea. In the mid-1970s, Saatchi & Saatchi created a commercial for Dunlop and in the process gave birth to a new kind of corporate advertising. Gone were the pompous, joyless, chest-beating claims on which corporate advertising had always been built. Instead, the Dunlop script set out to show how much the world depended on Dunlop's wide, but relatively unknown range of products, by having them disappear suddenly from a variety of different situations.

The scenes were played for laughs. For example, a Dunlop tennis umpire's chair disappears, leaving the umpire to drop to the ground minus his dignity. Firemen, aiming a working Dunlop hose at a fire, are left bewildered when the hose is suddenly not there. A ruddy-faced farmer finds himself losing his balance and landing in deep mud when his Dunlop wellington boots disappear. And so on. But, as with the dog, cat and mouse story, this presented a seemingly impossible challenge. Fortunately for the creative team, copywriter Andrew Rutherford and art director Ron Mather, one of the most talented and awarded directors, Roger Woodburn, rose to the challenge and delivered a groundbreaking commercial of great charm and the highest technical skill. As the Dunlop products all

disappeared so convincingly, the audience was treated to the work of a film-making magician.

In the late 1980s, art director Peter Gibb decided the Silk Cut cigarette campaign had got into a bit of a rut of still-life shots of pieces of purple silk with cuts in them – even though many were very imaginative. With his thinking no doubt influenced by the Saatchi company motto, Gibb came up with the possibility of using the mud men of Papua New Guinea. His idea was to have the purple silk stretched on a frame as a target to be 'cut' by spears. His executive creative director, Paul Arden, loved the idea and found the funds for Gibb to go off and shoot. Forget about client approval – shoot first and ask the question, 'Do you like it?', later.

The next issue was to find a photographer who would be right for the job. According to Gibb, Annie Leonard, whom he describes as 'the best art buyer I ever worked with', suggested Sebastião Salgado. He had recently had a collection of gritty photographs of miners working open-cast gold mines in his native Brazil published in *The Sunday Times* to great acclaim. Gibb considered Salgado 'a true genius' but said to Leonard that there was 'no way' he would agree to shoot an ad.

Clearly Leonard was not listening, and she somehow persuaded Salgado to take on the job, so Gibb and he flew off to Papua New Guinea for what Gibb describes as 'a truly amazing trip'. He returned with 2,500 wonderful pictures, not a dud among them.

The belief that anything was possible wasn't just restricted to the creative work itself. You might be forgiven for thinking that keeping a campaign appearing across the world and across all media on the same day a secret would probably be impossible. But it wasn't.

British Airways decided it was time to get the world flying again after the horrors of terrorist attacks such as the murder aboard the Achille Lauro cruise ship in 1985, as well as the Gulf War, which had resulted in a massive 30 per cent drop in airline passenger numbers. 'THE WORLD'S BIGGEST OFFER' was a spectacular promotion developed to tackle this decline. At its heart was an extraordinary giveaway: every seat on the airline's international services on 23 April 1991 would be given away free. All 50,000 of them.

To publicize the offer, a global campaign was developed to break on the same day in more than seventy countries around the world. This required the involvement of a significant proportion of all offices in Saatchi & Saatchi's global network. Obviously, to ensure maximum impact, the campaign had to remain an absolute secret. And, miraculously, it did.

One key step Saatchi & Saatchi took to keep the secret was to supply bogus advertisements to the press and only switch them for the real World's Biggest Offer ones at the eleventh hour. It's been calculated that, worldwide, some 500 million people read about the offer and 200 million saw it on TV – 5.7 million people entered the ballot for a free flight. But perhaps the most significant outcome of the campaign was the fact that passenger numbers were restored to their previous level within 120 days.

When Nick Crean received a call from Charles, who was on the way to Heathrow, late for his flight, informing him that he must 'stop the Concorde or you're dead!', he adopted the company motto to great effect. Crean called his BA contact and explained his problem. His contact, laughing, said, 'Give me a minute'. Crean waited nervously on the line. His contact came back. 'It's done. He's got fifteen minutes. We'll meet him and take him straight through.' According to Crean, Charles was impressed that Nick had in fact been able to successfully delay take-off.

An illustration of the boundless thinking that 'nothing is impossible' inspired came from one-time head of TV at Saatchi & Saatchi London, the late Jim Baker: 'Paul Arden called me to his office. "We want to project an ad on to the surface of the moon," he said. "Check it out, will you?"' Jim's enquires kept drawing blanks, or, more precisely, responses along the lines of 'Don't be daft!', 'Send me a letter of authority!', 'Stop wasting my time!' and 'Are you bonkers?!' This was a very rare occasion when something was not possible.

It seems appropriate to end this chapter with account director, Suzanne Douglas's memory of Paolo Ettorre's funeral in Rome: 'As the car began to slowly pull away with Paolo's coffin nestled among the flowers in the back, the sky suddenly exploded in a huge crack of thunder and brilliant lightning. The crowd burst into applause. Only Paolo could have pulled that off.'

Chapter 7

THERE'S NO BUSINESS LIKE NEW BUSINESS

The stories in this book often bear out just how important new business is to an agency. And it isn't exclusively about growth. To a degree, the adage that 'it isn't winning that matters, it's taking part' applies here. New business is a thermometer, showing how hot or not an agency is.

THE VERY FACT that an agency is invited on to a new business pitch list is a form of endorsement of the agency's status. Conversely, not making it on to pitch lists soon starts to give the impression that the agency isn't cool. It's cold.

Pitching for new business energizes the whole company. It's oxygen.

It's galvanizing. It inspires the freshest thinking, because the agency hasn't been worn down into producing, either consciously or subconsciously, only ideas that their intimate knowledge of an existing client tells them will be accepted.

Of course, this lack of intimate knowledge can lead to ideas that are so far outside a potential client's template for acceptability that the agency looks insane. Playing it safe has its risks too. As far as most creatives at Saatchi & Saatchi are concerned, to be told an idea of theirs is disappointing or ordinary is devastating. On balance, they'd probably prefer to be judged insane.

The person generally responsible for ensuring an agency is included on pitch lists is its new business or marketing director. Effective ones are a very rare breed.

It will come as no surprise that Saatchi & Saatchi's new business director at the outset was a man referred to frequently by John Tylee and Stefano Hatfield of *Campaign* magazine as 'the doyen': Graham Smith. Much of the work involves making cold calls to prospective clients. Many of the calls will end with the client's phone going dead suddenly, or with the same suggestion to 'go away' expressed verbally. Politely. Or robustly. Or possibly obscenely. But when Smith is asked about the need to have a very thick skin, he responds by saying, 'Not relevant. Don't even care if you [prospective client] ignore me or I you. On to the next. I'll get you in the end.' All of which suggests he does have a particularly thick skin after all.

Because another word doesn't exist, Smith would have to be described as a salesman, but it really doesn't do him justice. His sales pitch revolved around his view that 'I could introduce you to the possibility of having the most talented group of individuals there have ever been, working on your business – how could you possibly disagree with that?' His pitch reads like hyperbole but it didn't sound like it. And Richard Myers recalls just how effective Smith was during Saatchi & Saatchi's Lower Regent Street days when, without exaggeration, one would come back from lunch and ask what business had been won in that time.

Smith's phone-call targets were managed by a method that was called the Canal System. The Canal System was a metaphor for the new business development process. How the metaphor worked was this: once a client prospect (or barge) with money (coal) is put into the system (the canal) at one end, sooner or later they have to arrive at the port (Saatchi & Saatchi) as long as the lock-keepers (Saatchis' new business team) kept nudging them along. It was a logical numbers game – the more you put into the canal, the more you'd get out at the end.

Putting the Canal System into practice, Smith says he would call a prospective client and if the answer was 'no', he would take it to mean 'no – not at the moment', so he would then say he would call back on such and such a date, in three months' time. And he would call back on the exact day he said he would. This immediately indicated that you were someone who kept his word, you were highly professional, and that you were taking the prospective client's business seriously. A degree of trust was born.

According to Smith, rival agencies 'borrowed' the Canal System, but they often failed to keep the three-month promise to call back on the agreed date.

Sally De Rose (senior vice president, worldwide business development) describes another purpose of the system: 'It was to get prospects to come in and look at the agency's fantastic portfolio of work which they might otherwise not be able to do collectively in one batch. It was alluring.'

De Rose (and Ron Leagas) point out that the agency initially chose not to join the IPA (Institute of Practitioners in Advertising), thereby saving Smith from the inconvenience of their clear rule about not approaching other members' clients. A few years later, as De Rose recalls, Saatchi & Saatchi became the first agency to develop a worldwide computer system, with data development company Donovan Data Systems, 'to manage and coordinate its worldwide new business initiatives so everyone [in the network] knew what was going on, bang up to date'.

Another strategy of Smith's was to find out when a prospective client was going on holiday and, more to the point, when he or she was coming back.

Smith found that while lying by a pool somewhere, a client's thoughts would often turn to their agency, and how much they'd like to be with a different one. One of the first phone calls a client received when back from holiday would be from Smith. He also worked out, for similar reasons, that New Year was a fertile time to call.

Smith took a fearless approach to account conflict. 'We tried to break down conflict barriers – P&G versus Unilever versus Colgate Palmolive, for example. Clients would say, "Well, if you want any of our business you'll have to resign so and so." But we'd say, "Your accountants, auditors, legal advisors have accounts that would be regarded as conflicts, why are we different? Is it because the work we do is more important? If so, should we perhaps charge more for it?" All quite arguable stuff which led to the idea that "conflict is in the eye of the beholder".'

As Smith points out, British Airways, KLM, British Caledonian and Air New Zealand were all clients of Saatchi & Saatchi in Charlotte Street at the same time. More like an airport than an agency. 'And, memorably, both the Conservative Party and the Labour Party (but not for too long). As time went by, conflict became less of an issue – significantly, WPP Group now handles both P&G and Unilever.' Smith continues: 'I'm sure there are lots of other examples, brought about by some rational thought and subjectively, by the notion that

COMRADES CALL IN THE BROTHERS

"it doesn't matter that Saatchi & Saatchi have the account of one of our competitors, we want the best".'

Ask Smith what makes a good new business director and, modestly, he only concedes that, in his case, he just wouldn't let go of certain target clients.

Mike Parker was also an impressive new business getter. Like Smith before him, Parker had a sharp ear for hints and rumours floating around about client dissatisfaction at rival agencies. He also had an impressive black book of contacts that he constantly enlarged by never shrinking from making the most outrageous cold calls. He coped with rejection, after the briefest moment of disappointment, with an immovable, cast-iron belief that it was their loss, not his.

When Parker set up Team Saatchi, it was a natural home for accounts with conflicts in the main Saatchi & Saatchi agency. Prior to his Team Saatchi adventure, Parker describes a totally speculative trip, with a trade delegation, to Moscow. 'This led to a meeting with Gosteleradio, the state monopoly broadcaster across eleven time zones. Two young executives wanted advice on creating their first-ever commercial rate card and a deal was struck to bring them to London for a one-week media training session. In exchange, Saatchis were given five one-minute breaks of airtime to feature the first-ever western advertisers. Corporate ads for clients such as British Airways ("Face" commercial) and ICI ran, cut into their most popular programme, a weekly quiz show with a claimed audience of 60 million viewers. The news coverage Saatchis got was brilliant in the UK and the US. A headline in a British national newspaper read, "COMRADES CALL IN THE BROTHERS".'

Account director Andrew Horberry recalls his experience of this unusual piece of 'new business': 'We were ushered into an office in Gosteleradio's HQ in Moscow and introduced to senior executives. An interpreter explained that no business was to be discussed for the first half-hour, just small talk. Finally we got on to the important stuff, such as how much advertisers might be charged. A crucial factor was just how many millions of Soviet viewers there might be. Western advertisers, we explained, were used to paying a fee for every thousand viewers it could be proved watched the programming. "No problem," we were assured. "We have *two* methods of counting audiences." Which was two more than I was expecting. "Yes," said the head of Gosteleradio, proudly. "First, we count the number of television sets our factories produce." Hmmm. Unconventional, and not really going to fly with hardbitten media buyers in ad agencies across Europe and America.

"OK," I ventured "And your second method?"

"We count" – so far so good – "the number of letters our viewers send us!" There was clearly some work left to do on this, but at least Saatchis got some very good media coverage.'

The Russians must have been impressed too, because Parker received an unsolicited approach from the head of the Soviet Space Agency, General Dinayev, who was also the head of the Moscow Narodny Bank. 'Their idea, made clear by the rubbing together of thumb and finger, was to make money by flogging advertising space on the side of their rockets.' Later, the information that messages would be destroyed during blast-off led, indirectly, to Saatchi's involvement in Project Juno (a name invented by Saatchis).

The project was a private UK consortium formed to raise the money to pay the Soviet Union to train and put the first Brit into space. Saatchi & Saatchi were tasked with advertising, branding and managing the entire recruitment and selection process. The campaign, in 1989, including a press ad with the headline, **'ASTRONAUT WANTED. NO EXPERIENCE NECESSARY'** pulled in 13,000 responses, of which 500 were given detailed screening. Fifty then had full interviews and three were selected for training. And one, Helen Sharman, a chemist working at (appropriately perhaps) Mars, made it into space, aboard Soyuz TM-12, on 18 May 1991.

ASTRONAUT WANTED.
NO EXPERIENCE NECESSARY.

GLAVCOSMOS, the Soviet Space Administration, has offered a place to a British astronaut on a space flight in 1991.

Whoever is chosen will have had no experience because no Briton has ever flown in space ■ He or she will automatically write themselves into the history books ■ It is fitting that the flight is scheduled to take off on the 30th anniversary of Yuri Gagarin's historic first manned space flight on the 12th April 1991. It will be called the 'Juno' Mission.

The flight touches down eight days later.

The First ANGLO-SOVIET Space Mission. The eight days in space will be spent on the Soviet Space Station MIR from which the British astronaut will conduct scientific experiments ■ The MIR Orbital Space Station is a permanently operating 'laboratory in space' which has been orbiting earth since it first became fully operational in February 1988.

The British astronaut will become a full member of the Anglo-Soviet flight team fulfilling the tasks of an astronaut as well as conducting a series of scientific experiments ■ The mission is carrying no passengers.

The PURPOSE of the Mission. The aim is to conduct a series of scientific experiments in space which exploit the virtual absence of effective gravity in an orbiting spacecraft.

Most of the microgravity experiments will be carried out in order to advance our knowledge in basic science, others will demonstrate important principles in education and a few will test advances in space technology ■ The work will encompass biological experiments involving plants, cells, bacteria, and the astronaut.

Experiments in material science will include the growing of crystals, particularly of proteins, possibly the development of alloys, and the study of fluids under conditions which it is not possible to replicate on Earth.

The First COMMERCIAL Space Flight. The mission is the first commercial joint venture between the Soviet Space Administration and British industry.

In fact it's the first ever commercially supported manned space mission of its kind anywhere in this world. (Up until now commercial opportunities in space have been limited to unmanned satellite launches) ■ The mission will be funded by companies paying for the research capabilities of the mission as well as by sponsorship ■ (Previous flights from both East and West have been funded by their governments or space agencies and although it will be the first private enterprise space mission, it is operating with the full knowledge and consent of the respective governments).

This will without doubt be just the first of many commercial flights into space, as space becomes an increasingly viable product both academically and commercially.

How is The Mission FINANCED? The catalyst behind the mission is the Moscow Narodny Bank ■ This is a City of London bank which this year celebrates its 70th birthday as an established British incorporated bank.

It specialises in joint ventures and project finance and has provided the seed finance for the marketing and sponsorship raising campaigns ■ By co-operating closely with Licensintorg (foreign trade agents for Glavcosmos), the bank helped Glavcosmos enter commercial markets, internationally, for the first time ■ The Russian word for it is Perestroika.

The mission will raise £16M in revenue from the research capability and sponsorship ■ Commercial organisations will be able to sponsor the flight, the astronaut, or even supply products or services for the mission.

There will naturally be a programme of media events providing coverage of the mission around the world and it will also generate educational programmes, exhibitions and lectures.

Who's at The Mission CONTROLS? The selection process for the British astronaut, and the design and construction of much of the equipment which will be used to carry out the experiments devised by industry and universities, will be carried out at Brunel University.

The Brunel Institute for Bioengineering is one of the very few organisations in the UK with experience in the microgravity field and will act as the focus for this work.

space is open to both men and women.

Applicants will be aged 21-40 and possess a formal scientific training in either biology, applied physics, engineering or medicine, combined with good manual dexterity.

Successful applicants will have proven ability to learn a foreign language and have a high standard of medical fitness ■ They will also have the ability to work as a member of a team and communicate easily with people from a different background and culture.

Candidate assessment starts this month and at later stages will include a series of demanding medical, psychological, aptitude and stress tests.

The SELECTION Process. These will be completed by November 1989 when two final candidates will be selected to undergo a full schedule of training in the Soviet Union at the Gagarin Centre, Star City ■ One candidate will fly on the mission, whilst the other acts as back-up with duties in the running of control experiments at ground level which will be based at a laboratory close to the launch site.

How to APPLY. There is no coupon to clip and send. The Mission has employed MSL International (UK) Limited as recruitment consultants. They are at 32 Aybrook Street, London W1M 3JL ■ To obtain an application form please phone 01-224 2211 (16 lines) between 9am and 7pm on weekdays and 10am and 5pm at weekends ■ The line will remain open until Friday 14th July 1989.

The application closing date is Monday 24th July. Only applications on the formal application form will be considered.

Your OPPORTUNITY to Make History. The chance to become the first Briton in

JUNO
ДЖЮНО

THE FIRST ANGLO-SOVIET
SPACE MISSION ■

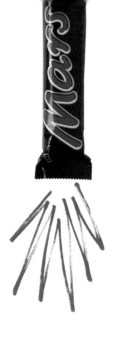

In fact, the consortium had failed to raise all the necessary funds, but Mikhail Gorbachev had intervened so the project could go ahead.

Most new business leads and pitches are rather more conventional, but they're still packed with incident, daring, clever thinking (both spontaneous and long-considered), mistakes and, occasionally, misbehaviour. An event that frequently precedes a new business pitch is the 'factory visit'. Saatchi & Saatchi were pitching for Club 18–30. Sylvia Meli was the senior planner assigned to the pitch. 'To familiarize ourselves with the product, a creative and I went to Ibiza, where we were to be looked after by the area rep. My objective was to interview as many holidaymakers as possible, and to go on a number of the trips organized for them, to demonstrate our commitment to the business and to develop an insightful creative brief.

'As soon as we arrived in the heat of Ibiza, the creative disappeared. I only saw him twice before we had to get on the plane home. Once waterskiing, and once late at night (when he wasn't alone). I decided to play the typical holidaymaker, only with less alcohol, no late-night door slamming, and sleeping in my own bed. After yet another beach game of pass the cucumber without using your hands (photographed by the area rep), I was beginning to feel my age (twenty-nine). At the next agency meeting, the photos appeared and I was awarded (embarrassed) the "devotion to client's business" internal award. And we won the pitch.'

Once a 'factory' has been visited, the creative work has to be done. However, in the case of Saatchi & Saatchi's pitch for British Leyland there was no factory visit and Charles Saatchi came up with the whole campaign in a matter of seconds. Saatchi & Saatchi had

How to convert an Audi into a British Leyland car with a scalpel and some glue.

pitched for Audi, unsuccessfully. Soon afterwards came the British Leyland pitch. Sean O'Connor says, 'Charlie got out the Audi ads we'd shown. He looked at them and then picked up a Magic Marker, crossed out "Audi", wrote "British Leyland", and then said, "Work them up." We won the account'. An early example of the benefits of recycling.

Something of a contrast to Charles's instant creative solution is the story of the pitch for TV-am, told by Tim Mousell (who later became director of international media at Saatchi & Saatchi UK). 'I'd just been elected to the board and felt full of my own importance, delighted to be involved in this major pitch. After the team had worked like dogs round the clock for the previous week or so, the time had come, the night before the pitch, for the agency's senior management to review our presentation.

'The large ground-floor theatre was an epidemic of deputy chairmen, department heads (of most disciplines), MDs, the chairman etc. All in all, about fifteen of Saatchi's most important, expensive and wisest people.

'My true role as a proud new board member soon became clear: legging it back and forth to typography, as the reviewing team came up with different changes and instructions.

'After a few hours, with the atmosphere getting tense and prickly, I returned from typography with the latest amendments to hear the pitch creative director, Adrian Kemsley, saying to the assembled group of the great and good,

"So you're telling me that on a forty-eight sheet poster, a housewife dressed in riot gear on a pair of roller skates, holding a green wobbly jelly is not an arresting sight?"

'The silence that followed was interrupted by me, convulsed in uncontrollable, hysterical laughter. Fortunately our chairman Bill Muirhead found it funny, too, slowly followed by the rest of the group.'

There have been occasions when other agencies competing for the same business have been very helpful to Saatchi & Saatchi. Accidentally. One story of this kind, told by strategic planner Steve Chinn, revolves around an IPA committee meeting being held at Saatchis one evening, hosted by the agency's vice chairman and executive planning director Marilyn Baxter:

'Senior people from other agencies were attending. One of them ran into one of his junior people in the corridor. Not questioning why "junior" was at Saatchis, and not realizing it was because he'd just moved to Saatchis, "senior" reeled off a list of changes he wanted made to the agency's pitch the next morning – charging "junior" with making the changes happen. We were pitching the same piece of business the next afternoon. On his way home that evening, "junior" popped into his old agency and left "senior" an envelope containing a photocopy of his leaving card. Of course, we didn't let "senior's" information influence our pitch...'

At a pitch for an additional piece of British Leyland business, Bill Muirhead discovered an art bag in the client's reception. According to account director Stephen Fox, 'Checking it out, Bill discovered it belonged to our main competitor. Either it had been left for later review or future presentation, but it didn't matter. A place was found to hide it. We won the business. We never actually discovered if the unfortunate loss of our rival's work was a factor.'

Pitching for another car account, Porsche, Bill Muirhead seized a ripe opportunity. Apparently, in an endearing piece of salesmanship, Bill walked the client to his office window and waved an expansive hand across the view of the agency car park, generously stocked with Porsches and other high-end cars and said,

'All this could be yours.'

Another pitch, another car account, this time Fiat, and one in which Charles showed great interest. Martyn Walsh and James Lowther's creative group, including Richard Myers, was working on the pitch one Sunday when the phone rang. 'It was Charles. He said, "I've got it! I've got the campaign line for you! I'm coming into the office!" We imagined it would be some time before Charles turned up from his home, so we settled back into trying to come up with our own ideas. What we forgot, of course, was that Charles had one of the very first car phones and in no time at all he burst into the room, very excited. "OK, it's...it's...oh fuck, I've forgotten it!" We never did get Charles's line. And nor did we get the Fiat account.'

New business pitches are often a test of wits and thinking imaginatively under intense pressure. In the pitch for Lesieur French dressings, Pete Watkins had to deal with a moment of great uncertainty for the prospective client. They told him they had never dealt with an agency before and didn't know how they would work with one, let alone get the best from it. Without hesitation he said,

'Don't worry. It's a very big and complicated machine, but you don't need to know how to work it, because I do!' Business won.

Watkins was on equally sharp form when he presented the agency's credentials to a very senior Japanese management delegation, visiting London. At the end of the presentation, one of them asked, 'Tell me, why are you called Saatchi *and* Saatchi?'

'Double the branding,' Watkins replied.

Perhaps inspired by these demonstrations of his spontaneity, Watkins decided to do the whole pitch for Mates Condoms, fronted by Richard Branson, spontaneously: 'Account director Penny Furniss had got us on the pitch list by cornering Branson at a press conference. The plan we hatched was we'd go down and meet Branson on his houseboat in Maida Vale, come up with ideas as we spoke and win him over with the immediacy of our brilliance. "We" being Paul Bainsfair, media planner Sheila Bowden and myself. What we actually did was, with art director Peter Gibb, come up with ideas we believed could fit most strategies. Gibb lightly pencilled them on a flip chart pad. During the meeting with Branson, Bainsfair suddenly took to the seemingly blank sheets of paper and "created" right there on the wooden floor of the houseboat.'

This mention of performance art segues neatly into some examples of theatre (or stunts) that Saatchi & Saatchi has frequently come up with to raise their pitches to new, more memorable levels. Team One's successful stunt of having someone in two places at once – New York and Los Angeles – is described in Chapter 4. President and CEO Patrick Pitcher recalls an imaginative, yet unsuccessful, piece of theatre deployed in Canada: 'We were trying to change the image of the agency from conservative to an acknowledged creative one. We pitched to a pharmaceutical company that produced an insect repellent. Our TV creative idea featured a naked man walking through a swamp. It also featured a pig, indicating that the repellent offered protection similar to pigskin. While the prospective clients were waiting in the agency's reception for the pitch, we'd arranged for a completely naked man with a live pig on a leash to walk nonchalantly through reception in full view of the clients. They didn't mention it in the pitch, not even when we took them through the script, featuring the naked man and the pig. We didn't win the business. We never saw them again.'

Unlikely as it sounds, a live pig plays a starring role in another Saatchi & Saatchi new business pitch theatrical interlude, this time in London. The product was a new Schweppes soft drink called The Raging Hog, and group account director Philippa Baldwin, who was managing the pitch, thought the meeting might benefit from the presence of a live raging hog. The creative team, John Pallant and Matt Ryan, were not too sure but reluctantly agreed.

Baldwin sourced a pig from a company that specialized in farm animals for photography and filming. A farmer's van duly arrived at the agency on the morning of the pitch with a pig on board. Baldwin says: 'As I approached the small van, it was rocking dangerously, and peering inside I saw an enormous sow in a very bad mood. The farmer confirmed that since giving birth she'd been quite violent. Not wanting the meeting to end in a lawsuit, I opted instead for her small piglet which the farmer had brought along too.

In the meeting room, the work had been laid out on the floor for the clients to finally review before making their decision. With the help of Roger Reynolds from maintenance, the piglet was herded along the corridor to the meeting-room door. When John Pallant was ready, the door was opened and in rushed the piglet to the screams of all the clients. He ran around the room leaving hoof marks and pig poo all over the work, and all over the carpet. We didn't win the business, but John wryly commented that "at least the clients hadn't shat on the work".' Gill Chapman, the long-time receptionist at 80 Charlotte Street, remembers dressing up as an airline stewardess and an army recruit for pitches, as well as wearing countless T-shirts with 'catchy slogans'.

Fate and chutzpah combined on one occasion to create a truly dramatic, but unintended pitch stunt. A Saatchi & Saatchi account man (who has been advised by the Metropolitan Police, for his own safety, never to allow his name to be disclosed in the context of this story) was driving to the office one morning when he witnessed the outcome of an armed robbery at a McDonald's outlet near the agency. He describes the situation he found himself caught up in: 'I hooted and accelerated towards the robber without thinking. He stopped and as he turned, I noticed a handgun that he raised in my direction. I braked and ducked. Glancing in the wing mirror, I noticed a security guard on the right. I heard a shot and felt a thud.

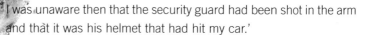

I was unaware then that the security guard had been shot in the arm and that it was his helmet that had hit my car.'

Spurred on by indignation ('How dare a man carry and fire a pistol in London?') X was determined to catch the offender. He grabbed a baseball bat from the boot of his car and chased the robber about a quarter of a mile to Great Portland Street Underground station. He saw the robber jump the barrier, which X did too. He then saw the robber on the opposite platform as a train pulled in. X dashed up the stairs and reached the other platform as the train doors were closing. 'I ran to the rear carriage and explained the situation to the guard there. I asked him to hold the train with the doors closed until the police arrived.' X dashed back up the stairs and was told the police were on their way. He ran back down to the platform only to see the train pulling away. 'I caught up with the train and thumped on the guard's door with the baseball bat, shouting at him to stop the train.' To X's relief, the guard did so.

'Armed police swarmed onto the platform. The train was reversed back into the station and I was walked along the side of the train by the police until I spotted the robber. The carriage doors were opened and the robber surrendered.'

Meanwhile, back at the agency, a new business pitch was underway. For McDonalds. The news of X's exploits had reached the agency and he recalls, 'I was told later that a note had been passed into the pitch about the robbery and the McDonalds clients were told something along the lines of, "We are so passionate about your business that one of our people has just foiled an armed raid on your local outlet and helped retrieve the stolen cash." We won the account.'

Perhaps the most celebrated stunt by Saatchi & Saatchi, certainly in London, was the pitch for the Toyota account. The determination to win the Toyota account in the UK inspired the agency to put a Toyota RAV 4 in their reception. The huge plate-glass window facing the street and measuring about eight metres by four metres had been removed to allow the car to be craned in. The client must have been impressed by this piece of theatre because the agency made it through to round two of the pitch process. The agency realized there was only one way to top this stunt. When the client team arrived for the follow up meeting there were two Toyota

Lobbying for business... Saatchi takes the client at its word and puts a second car in the reception area   HARRY BORDEN

Grand reception for Toyota used to steer work Saatchi's way

If at first you don't succeed, stick another Toyota in the reception area. That, at least, seems to be the philosophy at Saatchi and Saatchi, the well-known car showroom in Charlotte Street.

When the Toyota client first went to see Saatchi, the agency had placed a mere one Toyota (MR2, red) in the lobby.

"It was Pete Watkins's idea to show that we were really serious about the product," Saatchi's joint managing director, David Kershaw, says.

"It wasn't easy. We had to move all the glass from the front window, which is reinforced for security reasons [one wonders why] to get it in," he adds.

"When the client arrived and finally told us we were on the shortlist, he said 'When the top nobs come in, you'll have to have two Toyotas in reception'. We took him at his word and brought in another MR2. It took ten men to take the window out again, with all the agency staff standing around and watching.

"We showed that we're a 'can-do' agency and that we do listen to clients," Kershaw says.

The car stunt obviously paid off for Saatchi — it was awarded the Toyota business this week.

The cars in front of the reception desk are Toyotas.

MR2 sports cars in reception. The business was won.

There have been times when meticulous attention to detail has taken a back seat. Bill Muirhead is famously considered very laid back, although, generally speaking, this is a wholly misleading impression. David Williams (later CEO of Saatchi & Saatchi Warsaw) recalls a successful pitch he did with Muirhead for a pharmaceutical company. 'As I presented for twenty minutes on the consumer benefits of flu vaccinations, Bill spent the entire time at the other end of the table making faces, yawning and deliberately trying to put me off. It was a nightmare trying not to laugh whilst talking about the risk of the elderly dying. At the end, Bill said, "Wow! Where did you get those stats?" No, he hadn't read the pitch presentation at all.'

Terry Bannister and Roy Warman approached a pitch for Cinzano across Europe with similar nonchalance. Pete Watkins put the pitch together with account supervisor Tim Nicholls after seeking lots of advice from various people around the agency who ran international business. 'I had never handled anything international and this was way beyond anything I'd done before. I went to see Roy and Terry and showed them this plan of how the Saatchi empire across Europe planned to handle the business. They looked at the cover, not the contents and said, "Do you think it'll work?"

"Yes," I said.

"Good," they said. At which point they asked Tim to stand on the table so they could take a look at his socks – which were ridiculously fashionable. We didn't win the pitch, but Tim and I both learnt a lot about the logistics of international business and perhaps more importantly, about confidence and trust.'

No matter how cleverly pitches are approached, there's always the risk of bad luck or carelessness derailing the best-laid plans. Pitches generally start with the agency's credentials and an introduction of the agency team to people in the room and a brief description of their experience and reasons why they'd be perfect to work on the prospective client's business.

Sylvia Meli describes something of the lead up to this key meeting: 'You were expected to become a near expert on a market sector, new to you, within days. Staying up all night on a pitch was not uncommon. And so it was for a pitch to the California Raisin Advisory Board. After horrendously long hours of preparation, the pitch got under way, headed up by the [garrulous] group account director Mark Cunningham. After two hours the client said, "That was real, real interesting, but I have to go now to catch my plane back to the US." As I explained afterwards to my crestfallen, but by now worldwide raisin market expert junior planner, "Mark enjoyed talking about Saatchis and himself so much he didn't actually get on to talking about the client's business and didn't mention raisins once."'

On another occasion, Saatchi & Saatchi had made it onto a longlist to pitch for a pharmaceutical account, and the agency would make the shortlist by showing the client and their consultants what it would be like to work with the agency. The strategic planner on the pitch was Steve Chinn. 'We decided to run an ideas workshop, involving role play to get some real insight about a problem as awkward as the one we would face if we won the business. We chose erectile dysfunction. We insisted, against their will, that the consultants, a husband and wife team, join in. As the evening progressed, he got more and more choked up and redder. She, meanwhile, got more sarcastic and emotional. Eventually, he left for their hotel but she insisted on going out for a drink. Or ten. Guess what she revealed? We didn't make the shortlist.' Possibly not a cock-up (in one respect at least) but definitely a blunder.

Saatchi & Saatchi's pitch for BT, however, can certainly be described in less than favourable terms. It's a frequently told story but it's worth repeating here. Having made the loved-by-all Stephen Hawking commercial for BT Corporate, Saatchis' reward was to be invited to pitch for their retail business (Call Stimulation, as it was known). Account man Stef Tiratelli describes what happened: 'On the day, we had managing director David Kershaw, Jeremy Sinclair, Simon Dicketts, account director Nick Hurrell and myself. On the client side, a whole host of familiar faces including Adrian Hosford (director BT customer communications), Robert Bean (worldwide head of advertising and media quality) and the tall, bespectacled head of campaign strategy, Tim Evans, who had a fearsome reputation and was a ruthless critic of creative work.

'The presentation went OK but not great. At the end, we were asked by the client if we would leave the room so they could gather their thoughts before going on to the next pitching agency. After the clients left, we gathered in the pitch room for a little post-mortem. I went round to where the clients had been sitting to check their notepads for any feedback about our presentation. What stopped me in my tracks was a note that read: "There'll be trouble from the cunt in the corner with the glasses." What? Nick Hurrell was the only one on our side wearing glasses, but he hadn't been in the corner, nor had he made any trouble, and no reasonable person would ever describe him as a cunt. When I read out the note there was a long silence before a voice piped up,

"Oh God! It was me. I wrote that!"

The voice belonged to David Kershaw. He'd written it in response to Jeremy Sinclair, sitting next to him, who'd asked him if there were any hostile clients on the other side of the table.

'That night, I met some friends in Soho. They were from Simons Palmer, the agency BT had gone to next. They burst out laughing when I walked in. They explained that the BT clients had said as they sat down for the pitch, "Try not to call the client a cunt in the presentation. Saatchi did and they didn't get away with it!"' Saatchis didn't win the pitch, unsurprisingly, but the story ran and ran. BT themselves had a field day with it.

A few weeks later Tiratelli was kept waiting for ages at BT's offices ahead of a presentation. Finally, Tim Evans appeared saying, 'Sorry I'm late, but at least the cunt in the glasses isn't here today.' But Tiratelli reckons BT's best response came later that year at a big set-piece meeting in the agency with seven or eight clients and all Saatchis' management. 'As the clients entered the meeting room they lined themselves up behind the chairs, arranging themselves in height order, ranging from a six-foot-seven campaign manager on the left to the diminutive Tim Patten on the right. On the count of three, they all took a pair of glasses from their top pockets, put them on, and in unison declared, "I'm the cunt with the glasses!" David Kershaw was promoted to chairman shortly afterwards.'

As well as a plethora of clever pitches and engineered opportunities, Saatchis also enjoyed their fair share of new business shoo-ins. One example was Silk Cut, although it wasn't the simplest of shoo-ins. According to account director Neil Chalmers, 'What nobody knew when the new business juggernaut rolled up and unloaded the Silk Cut account at Charlotte Street, was that sometime before, Stuart Cameron, the chairman of Gallaher, had had dinner with Maurice and Charles. They had sold him on the idea that Charles had originally when a copywriter at Colletts, taking

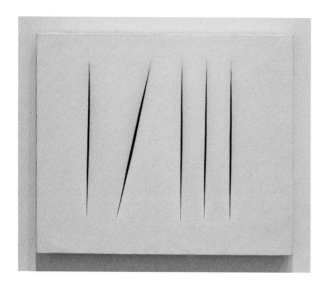

Lucio Fontana's piece, which probably inspired the Silk Cut campaign.

artist Lucio Fontana's cuts in material from his famous series of paintings and applying that concept to purple silk, simply underscored with a health warning in order to heavily brand and bring up to date what had, up until then, been seen as a bit of a medicinal, lady's smoke. To ensure ultimate security on the development of the campaign, only Paul Arden and Jeremy Sinclair knew what was going on. The account group, which I had joined to specifically work on the Silk Cut business, and the client team blithely proceeded to develop strategies, do research, plan media and develop advertising with all the usual attendant struggles, arguments, frustrations and minor triumphs: oh yes, and a lot of lunches.

After about six months, by which time the client team was beginning to show some signs of frustration, despite the lunches, the account group got a call from Charles's PA, Stafford Everard, to come to the sixth floor where Charles had something to show us. Twenty minutes later, after having only been marginally distracted by Charles's deaf schnauzer Lulu bumping continually into the glass wall of the executive meeting room, the entire gamut of subjects for the first phase of the launch campaign and a whole lot more had been revealed. Charles told us that it was now our job to sell the campaign that the client team would have no idea was coming.

'A meeting was set up, and serried Gallaher ranks sat but not, of course, including the co-conspirator chairman, facing the similarly serried ranks of the agency, with two chairs reserved for Maurice and Charles which remained empty. Group account director John Emerson delivered a superb presentation performance and the assembled clients, Peter Wilson, Mike Perry, Nigel Northridge and a slack handful of brand managers could do little but be swept away.

But the fall-out was quick and none too pleasant, with Emmo (John Emerson) getting the "Spanish Archer" from the UK business two days later for being the visible leader of the deception.'

Strategic planner David Keig's recollection adds a little spice. 'Somehow Charles and Maurice had engineered a pitch for this particular Gallaher brand. The rumour was that Charles had already pre-sold a campaign to Gallaher directors. I had the task of pre-testing the creative work. A courier arrived with beautifully crafted artwork. Everyone in the research group was impressed but there were problems with the idea. The work had a sinister feel to it – ripped or torn silk, rather than cut silk. Later, the pitch presentation was a little odd. All of the Gallaher brand management seemed at pains to say how much they loved the work, while the marketing director was almost purring as the work was shown. He had seen the work before and let it be known within Gallaher how impressed he was with it. My report had been altered. Findings were changed to almost the direct opposite of what I had written. Rather than say that some people found the images sinister and violent, it now stated that no one saw them that way.'

Another less than straightforward new business pitch involved US-born Saatchi account director Peter Levitan who was now based in London. He received a call saying Maurice Saatchi would like to see him at Saatchis' Berkeley Square 'cathedral'. 'Maurice tells me we're pitching Adidas's global business, that I will run the pitch and, if we win it, I will run the account. Cool. Then I meet Charles who is going to manage the creative direction. Cool again. Oh, and it's a "shoo-in" as Robert Louis-Dreyfus is the new Adidas CEO and Louis-Dreyfus had been Saatchi & Saatchi's worldwide CEO. Robert confirmed our future by saying,

"You have the business unless you fuck up the pitch."

'A few weeks into what became the most expensive pitch ever, the pitch team, apart from Charles, Paul [Arden] and Jeremy [Sinclair], were a bit concerned. The old-guard creatives thought they had a handle on youth culture and came up with the campaign, "Sport is God". This was rolled into a pitch film that dazzled with images like baby seals being clubbed, juxtaposed against athletes

winning. Bloody baby seals! Can you imagine the look on the Adidas faces during the pitch? Am I running the Adidas global account?' He wasn't, because even when a shoo-in presents itself, you can still trip over your own feet.

But perhaps the smartest variation on the shoo-in was devised by John (later Lord) Sharkey. According to account man Ian McAteer, Sharkey persuaded the agency's unhappy Avis client not to put their business out to pitch. He argued that the agency was like five or six agencies in one so he could offer the client a competitive internal pitch. The Avis client was persuaded, and the agency retained the business. Later the same method was adopted successfully in similar circumstances for Flymo and Sky.

Fundamental to all Saatchi & Saatchi new business efforts has been the pure determination to win, and the refusal to take 'no' for an answer. Group account director John Rudaizky illustrates this very clearly with three of his new business experiences. 'We were told we probably had no chance of winning the £20 million Visa International account and we were knocked out of the pitch process midway. But with some internal inspiration drawn from the Muhammad Ali film, *When We Were Kings*, we got ourselves reinstated and went on to win in the final round.

'We were also knocked out of the pitch for Adams Children's Wear, being told our creative work wasn't right. So we did some more. And won. We were given no chance of winning the £50 million Sony account right at the start, apart from a window to submit credentials, alongside nine other agencies. We spent six months, fighting each day, and finally won the business.'

Apparently, worldwide CEO Kevin Roberts couldn't keep in check his competitiveness and desire to win new business when he and Richard Hytner (deputy chairman worldwide and football fanatic) had an exclusive personal tour of Real Madrid's Santiago Bernabéu football stadium. It was arranged (with some chutzpah) by Antonella Broglia, the managing director of Saatchi & Saatchi Spain. She told them: 'There will be a short meeting after our very special walk on the pitch and our sit-down in the dugout. You will meet Manuel Mendía, Real Madrid's vice president, so you will get the chance to thank him in person for this once-in-a-lifetime opportunity, and Kevin,' she added knowingly, 'please do *not* ask him for the business. I have promised Manuel that this is a purely personal visit to fulfil one of Richard's lifetime dreams.'

'Understood,' said Roberts, before whispering to Hytner, 'Play our cards right Richard, *mon brave*, and there'll be season tickets here for life for the two of us!'

'Good afternoon, Señor Mendía. Thank you so much for showing us round the Bernabéu. You've made Richard a very happy man,' said Roberts in the boardroom.

'Now remind me why you are not working with Saatchi & Saatchi?'

The need to win new business became vital when the Saatchi brothers left their namesake agency in 1995. At the time, Adam Crozier and Tamara Ingram were made joint MDs and the new business approach they immediately adopted was a 'like for like' strategy in order to replace the business that left with the brothers. The agency was able to go to prospective clients in the same sectors and say, justifiably, that they had all the expertise and market knowledge the prospect needed. The strategy had to succeed in order to indicate that the agency was doing more than just surviving, it was prospering. The need to prevent downward momentum was paramount. In turn, it had to counter Maurice and Charles's suspected strategy of destabilizing Saatchi & Saatchi to such an extent that they would be called back to rescue the company.

Crozier was responsible for winning Rothmans to replace Silk Cut (lost to M&C), and Comet to replace Dixons Currys (lost to M&C). Saatchi & Saatchi's US operation took the lead in the successful pitch to replace the British Airways account (lost to M&C) with Delta Airlines. As a matter of interest, these new business replacements came much quicker than normal. (Incidentally, when British Airways first threatened to move their account to Maurice and Charles's new outfit, Crozier called their bluff. He suggested they should go ahead and leave immediately, knowing full well that the brothers didn't have the means to handle the account.)

Saatchi & Saatchi people will go to any length, and make any sacrifice to win new business, Charles Saatchi included, although he made it a rule never to meet clients. There were two rare occasions, however, when he broke this rule. Deputy chairman, the late John Spratling, recalled how a senior board member had agreed to meet and give the agency advice before it pitched for his company's business: 'Charles, Jeremy Sinclair and I rehearsed daily, three different strategic approaches, the resulting creative campaigns and the extensive rationales. After two rehearsals each day, all seemed well, and word-perfect. But when the client arrived, Charles went immediately off script and said,

"I can't wait, why don't I just show you the creative idea we recommend?"'

When Saatchi & Saatchi won the Sainsbury's supermarket account there was one small hitch. Account director Ian McLaren explains: 'Sir John Sainsbury insisted on meeting Charles, saying, "My name is over my door – I want to meet the man whose name is over yours!" Well, Charles agreed rather reluctantly to meet Sir John, and the deal was sealed.'

One of the highest profile new business wins in the Saatchi & Saatchi story was British Airways. Charles and Maurice's PA at the time, Andrew Green, saw it happen. 'In the summer of 1982 Maurice often spoke to Lord King, then the new chairman of British Airways. I didn't think much of it, as he often spoke to industry bigwigs in the course of his day. But one day after he had met with market researcher Liz Nelson [the co-founder and the 'N' of what became TNS, the global market research company], he asked me if I could ring her with my home address, so she could send something through to me. He said it was too confidential to be routed through the company's despatch department.

'A few days later a thick envelope arrived through my door in Tottenham. I opened it and it contained a sheaf of drawings and a write-up of some interviews with frequent air travellers. I duly delivered the package to Maurice.

'He and Charles spent the next few days working intensely with few interruptions – on what, I did not really know. But it was soon clear that this was their pitch for Saatchi & Saatchi to take over the advertising duties for what was to be a new and improved British Airways. And it was really them who did everything, from commissioning the research to writing the proposal.

'I remember the agency's managing director Tim Bell racing up to see Maurice the day he saw the announcement in *Campaign* that we had picked up what was an enormous and very high-profile account. It was a funny way to do business, but you can't help but admire them for the result.'

Tim Bell's version of being kept in the dark certainly doesn't involve reading about the win in *Campaign*. Very soon after he had successfully re-pitched to retain the agency's British Caledonian (airline) account, Bell received a call from the head of communications at British Airways, suggesting they meet since they would be working together. Bell played along, but then confronted Charles, who denied it. A second call to Bell from another senior British Airways executive followed. He had another face-to-face with Charles, who again denied it, suggesting Bell ask Maurice, who, after a while, admitted it.

However the account was given to Bill Muirhead to run, even though BA's John King (who, incidentally, was a personal friend of Bell's), Robert Ayling and Colin Marshall all wanted Bell to run their account. According to Bell, it seemed clear that Charles and Maurice wanted him to leave the agency.

Saatchi & Saatchi certainly believe in celebrating new business successes and group account director Sue Beazley recalls a particularly splendid event. 'Charles Saatchi was very pleased with my group's consecutive new business successes. So much so that he gave me a budget to "take the group out". This ended up as a trip to a celebrated restaurant near Caen. We gathered at Luton Airport with a case of champagne and brandy, and piled onto a Trislander – like flying in a cigar tube. On arrival at Caen, we turned down the offer of a local tour so we could get straight down to the business of drinking and eating.

'We started with Calvados and champagne cocktails and worked our way through a tasting menu of Normandy specialities,

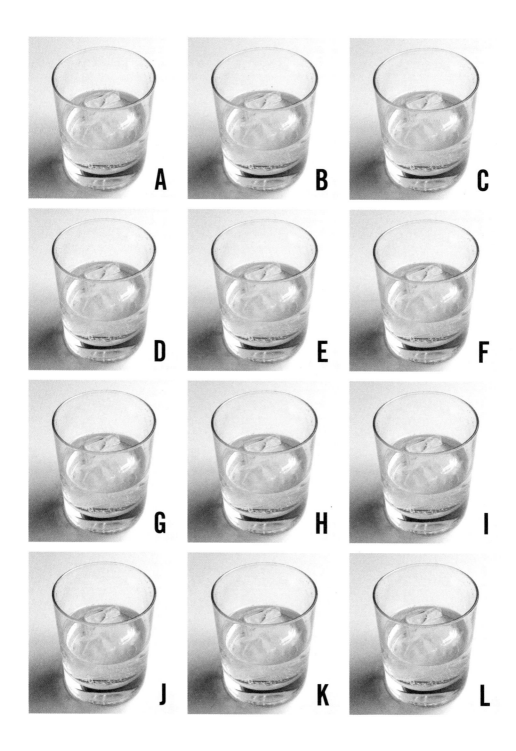

before being poured back onto the plane. Back at Luton, [account handler] John Truscott was so pissed he couldn't find his way through the automatic doors between the arrivals area and the concourse. I drove home.'

When Saatchi & Saatchi won the Tanqueray Gin account, during a mutual celebration with the client, Roy Warman pronounced himself an expert on gin. The client protested that the differences were slight across not only their own brands, but the market as a whole. Warman demanded a blind taste test, so various brands were wheeled in and the room embarked on an ice-breaking indulgence of gin. As Pete Watkins notes, 'Roy got them all right, teaching me what I would continue to learn: that confidence is all.' So this wasn't simply a celebration; it confirmed for the clients that they'd chosen the right agency.

Arguably, Saatchi & Saatchi's most famous new business win was the Conservative Party. But it will surprise no one to learn that there have been several versions of how the account was won.

According to Tim Bell, Saatchi & Saatchi's appointment was driven by Gordon Reece, the Conservative Party's director of publicity at the time. He recognized that the party needed experts in print and TV advertising, and Saatchi & Saatchi met that criterion.

Reece spoke to Maurice Saatchi. Maurice then consulted Bell, on holiday in Barbados, about the business. Bell readily admits he wasn't keen on taking on the account and told Maurice so. His advice was ignored and Bell returned to find he would be running the agency's new Conservative Party account 'under Maurice's leadership'.

Bell recalls the first meeting at Saatchis' offices in Charlotte Street, when the party chairman Lord Thorneycroft's driver parked next to Charles's Jeep Cherokee which sported huge 'roo bars. Lord Thorneycroft commented, 'He must have lots of trouble with kangaroos in St Johns Wood.'

Bell's long and friendly relationship with Margaret Thatcher is well documented. According to Bell, she took the view in those early days that 'we knew what we were doing – "have an idea and back it"'. She also reportedly said, 'If you try and tell me how to run the country, it will not be appreciated and you will be made to regret it!'

Beware.
Saatchi drivers
have ears.

Perhaps the greatest irony about Saatchi & Saatchi's most momentous new business win was how easy it all was and what little effort went into winning it. As Bell says, 'No creative work was presented. It was a shoo-in!'

And when it isn't a shoo-in, it's worth recording that a Saatchi & Saatchi pitch didn't end when the prospective clients left the agency meeting. As account man Ian McAteer explains, 'They would be driven away in one of the agency's taxis, Jet Cars. Inevitably, the clients would chat, the Jet driver would listen, and then call in with the "feedback" he'd gathered about how the pitch had gone.'

The final thought on pitches has to be Paul Arden's:

'Never put your best people on new business. Put on your luckiest.'

Chapter 8

THE MISSIONARY POSITION

Two things ensured that Saatchi & Saatchi would not be staying at home in the UK. One was the declared ambition to be the biggest advertising agency in the world. The other was the wholehearted embrace of globalization.

PERHAPS UNSURPRISINGLY, for Saatchi & Saatchi the theory of globalization was well and truly embraced, but the practice was lagging a little behind as (then account director) Rosemary Lloyd (formerly West) remembers: 'Saatchis had just announced to the world (or to the press at least) that they were *the* global agency, claiming that global advertising can be as creative as the local variety.

'Not long after the announcement, the Campbell Soup Company was having its major marketing conference in London, so they asked Saatchis to do a presentation with the argument for global advertising. Meanwhile, the local argument would be delivered by the highly creative London agency CDP – this in the days when they were producing classic ads for Cinzano with Joan Collins and Leonard Rossiter, Heineken "Refreshes the Parts", Fiat "Hand Built by Robots" and many more. So, not an easy task to prepare a persuasive argument as to why global advertising can be as creative. But Saatchis had obviously prepared the argument in full in order to go public with it. So off I went to [head of strategy] David Miln to get the Saatchi global presentation. The presentation didn't exist. I was left with the task of inventing it.'

Clearly, if global ambitions were to be achieved, Saatchi & Saatchi had to set up a global agency network. And if they wanted their brand to be consistent throughout the world, this would entail shipping both their attitude and their culture overseas. But how do you export a corporate culture? How do you combine diplomacy with compulsion? How do you build an empire without behaving like imperialists and generating nothing but resentment? Unless you get it right, the chances of your being welcomed with open arms are about as remote as some of the places you're hoping to set up shop in.

It's probably fair to say that Saatchi & Saatchi's culture at the time was not particularly international in outlook. In most respects it was very British, which is one way of saying there was a tendency to regard most foreigners with either bemusement or in terms of stereotypes.

Alban Lloyd, one-time chairman of Saatchis Europe, tells the story of the account director who breezed into his office in Charlotte Street, all Armani glasses, unstructured suit and equally unstructured mockney grammar.

" 'Ere Alb, we got an agency in Milan?"

"Yes," I said.

"What's the geezer's name what runs it?"

"Robert Lasagna," I replied.

"Waaayyy! Cannelloni! Spaghetti! Etc!"

Since I'd lived in Italy a while, I was used to this sort of fun but it bored me slightly. He then said, "Does the geezer speak any English?"

Now Robert's mother was English, he went to school in England, and is perfectly bilingual. But I wasn't going to tell Mr Unstructured this, so I said he couldn't speak a word of English, "So you'll have to use pidgin English with him. What are you going to Italy for?"

"British Airways account," he said.

"So," I said, "simple – stick your arms out like wings and say something like, 'Me Fred Bloggs. You Robert Lasagna. We talk about BA (whilst swinging arms about)'."

Apparently Robert (who later went on to become a senator in the Italian Upper House, the Senate of the Republic) took it in his stride and said, "Would you care for a small sherry and then we can have a spot of lunch, what?"

On his return, the account director came into my office. "You shit!" he said. "You told me the geezer didn't speak no English!"

"Blimey!" I said. "That's incredible, we only sent him the Linguaphone records a month ago!"'

Perhaps the agency could, at times, be shamefully typical of a British attitude that prevailed at the time. To illustrate, Neil Kennedy tells the story of Saatchi & Saatchi's new business pitch for the Spanish Tourist Board account. 'The key client was a short, fat, bald-headed Spaniard, the Minister of Tourism, but every regional tourism director was there too. At the pitch, the message arrived to say the minister was delayed, but the pitch should start without him.

Tim Bell (who only ever went to Mustique or Barbados for his holidays) was playing to the gallery and buttering up each regional director in turn, saying how much he loved his holidays in "AndaluTHia" and "BarTHelona" and "ValenTHia" etc – really overdoing the Spanish "TH" pronunciation of a "C". The boss client now arrived, wearing a white suit. Instantly, Roy Warman passed Tim a note that read, "Who's the short, fat, bald-headed THunt in the white suit?" Bell was laughing so much he had to leave the room!'

Pete Watkins reports another linguistic laugh he and his account team enjoyed during their dealings with the French company Lesieur. Day-to-day contact was with two attractive female clients. At one meeting they asked Watkins and his account handling colleagues, Tim Nicholls and Paul Hammersley, to 'Fuck us on the table.' What they were actually saying, with a heavy French accent, was 'focus on the table', which had the ads on it. According to Watkins they also insisted on calling Paul Hammersley, 'Paula Mersley'.

The odds might have seemed stacked against Saatchi & Saatchi succeeding in building another British empire. However, success came through a combination of self-belief bordering on (and occasionally crossing the border into) arrogance, and a number of people, such as Alban Lloyd, who were blessed with a more worldly sensitivity. Other key facets of Saatchi & Saatchi culture including fearlessness, ingenuity and, of course, chutzpah, were also instrumental in creating a global brand.

Charles and Maurice Saatchi's PA Nick Crean was asked (with Simon Mellor's help) 'to analyze US agencies Saatchis might want to acquire. Figures analyzed, creative work sneakily got hold of and reviewed. I was given the task then of phoning the CEOs and getting appointments for Maurice to meet with them. It was incredibly exciting, few had heard of Saatchi & Saatchi. So I simply explained who we were and stated that we were interested in buying them, hence the need for a meeting!

'Intrigue and greed, it worked every time.'

Few people played a more significant role in building Saatchi & Saatchi's global empire than Roy Warman and his management partner Terry Bannister, who were promoted to lead the international division after running the UK agency very successfully for a number of years. Although their modus operandi has been characterized as a little eccentric, controversial even, they were highly effective.

As Bannister says, 'Certainly we were tough at times, but our initial and follow-up approach was to give encouragement to those who signed up to the Saatchi culture. Our "attack mode" was reserved for those who didn't accept that, having sold their agency, a little adaptation to a new way of doing things was required.'

Warman cites the takeover, in 1986, of New York agency DFS (Dancer, Fitzgerald, Sample). 'The resistance we faced from the Americans when they'd taken the money and then did everything possible to be obstructive in wanting to understand and accept Saatchi culture. It was a horrible time. The place [DFS] was a mess.

No way could the job of managing the change be done without ruffling a few feathers. It was always going to be difficult – we were astounded by the resistance of the US management to the purchase. They made heaps more money than we ever did and never showed, to us at least, the slightest intention of wanting to become a true Saatchi agency.'

When Saatchi & Saatchi bought Barcelona's star agency RCP (also in 1986), Bannister and Warman faced resistance again from Casadevall and Pedreño (the 'C' and 'P' in RCP). They were on the receiving end of a lengthy diatribe about the principle of Catalan independence, and that RCP would not recognize instructions from London until the end of their earn-out five years hence. According to Bannister, of all the agency sellers, RCP took the promise of operational autonomy (given by Saatchi's acquisition team without reference to the operators, Warman and Bannister) most literally. 'They effectively believed they were in a deferred-integration situation for five years, getting to cherry-pick the bits of the Saatchi network that suited them whilst still free to act independently, even against the interests of the network, if it suited them.'

Warman and Bannister, in an attempt to open Casadevall and Pedreño's eyes to the reality of the situation and the consequences of the deal they had made, pointed out to them with some elegance that 'you've taken the King's shilling'. Casadevall and Pedreño refused to understand, feigning a complete linguistic failure.

Bannister's response to suggestions that he and Warman's methods may have been too critical and aggressive is very clear. 'Blanket criticism was never our way because if we created a hostile atmosphere at the outset it was much harder to get the attitudinal changes needed for success. The criticism came later when there was evidence of inflexibility, indolence or incompetence.'

This is neatly illustrated by the account of Peter Cullinane (who would ultimately become COO of Saatchi & Saatchi Worldwide) of his agency being bought by Saatchi & Saatchi and how it was devoid of any questionable behaviour by the people from London.

'It was demonstrated first when Saatchi & Saatchi agreed to buy our (then locally owned) agency in New Zealand, even though they owned a perfectly good one already! But it wasn't a great one and we (in all modesty) were.

'The opportunity to live up to another great Saatchi-ism coined by Jeremy Sinclair –

"It's good to be big, it's better to be good, but it's best to be both."

– proved too enticing. And so the deal was done in complete secrecy in London with Roy Warman, Terry Bannister, Richard Humphreys [then CEO of Saatchi & Saatchi Advertising International] and, my now great good friend, Alban Lloyd. On our side the deal was led by Terry King, John Swan, Neville Goldie and me as the "whipper snapper". Two months after we made contact, the deal was done and the New Zealand ad world awoke to the announcement that Saatchi & Saatchi had, overnight, become the country's biggest and most creative agency. That came as a particular shock to the current Saatchi agency staff who we got to meet for the first time on the day of the announcement.'

Cullinane then recounts what happened a few months later: 'I remember attending a budget review meeting with Roy and Terry. Our numbers were not looking promising. I was taken out by them for a few pints late in the evening (one pint is enough to get me tipsy) then led back to their shared office for the interrogation. This took the form of Terry asking the hard questions while Roy practised his golf swing with a driver just behind me...I'm pretty sure I promised to improve the numbers.'

Perhaps some people found Warman and Bannister's management style difficult at times but as Bannister points out, 'one of the things that would seem scarcely credible now is that, in all the years that we ran companies for Saatchi, we produced year-on-year profit growth for the advertising businesses, never a decline'. Above all, they helped Saatchis achieve the seemingly impossible ambition to be the world's biggest agency, which finally happened in 1986 after the acquisition of Bates.

So their occasionally 'different' way of working should not be allowed to overshadow Warman and Bannister's achievements in establishing and managing Saatchi & Saatchi's highly successful global network, having previously run the UK agency, and before that as, respectively, the original agency's media director, and as one of the most effective, revenue-building account directors in the company's history. Paul Bainsfair is keen to see a balanced view of Warman and Bannister in this book:

'It's true to say their approach was less than conventional, but I believe it would be wrong to give the impression that they were irresponsible. They were absolutely critical in creating the "nothing is impossible" culture in Charlotte Street. Without them, the agency would not have achieved anywhere near the same success. They were truly effective leaders.'

And in Sir Martin Sorrell's opinion, 'Roy Warman and Terry Bannister were a formidable combination.'

One particular endorsement for Warman and Bannister's talents came from Charles Saatchi apparently. He announced to them that the company was going to buy Midland Bank. Warman and Bannister, somewhat bemused, asked Charles the reasonable question – who would run the bank? 'We thought you might,' Charles replied. It could be argued that Warman and Bannister's way of working was simply representative of the part of Saatchi culture that was fuelled by boundless self-belief, the pleasure derived from being seen as maverick outsiders, the overwhelming urge to succeed and the general disregard for rules and other inconveniences.

The smoothness of the purchase (at least) of Cullinane's agency in New Zealand contrasts sharply with experiences of establishing offices elsewhere in the world. Gerry Nagle sets the scene for the Saatchi & Saatchi start-up in Saudi Arabia: 'The challenge was how to open an agency in the Kingdom of Saudi Arabia when your parent company name, Saatchi, means watchmaker and your parent company principals come from an Iraqi Jewish background. And, by the way, do this when coalition forces were in Saudi fighting Iraq in the first Gulf War!'

Who's a pretty
obscene boy then?

In February 1990, Nagle had attended a Procter & Gamble review meeting in Dublin. Having a drink after the (successful) meeting, Werner Goerke and John (now Lord) Sharkey (deputy chairman of Saatchi & Saatchi International) mentioned the challenge of looking after P&G in Jeddah, to which Nagle said, 'Throw my name in the hat!' Within two weeks Nagle was in London, 'with my good friend Simon Goode, getting an orientation on the business, and then it was off to Jeddah with Sharkey to meet the client. We had a good meeting and then met my new staff. Two account people, a secretary, no creatives and a parrot named Toby who could only say, "Fuck off, Mavis!" The parrot's owner, Tom, had trained the bird to say this when he left it with his mother-in-law, when he moved to Saudi and was waiting for papers to bring his bird from the US to Jeddah. Poor Mavis.'

Within a few weeks of arriving, Nagle realized the agency was a mess. He got permission to get in an accountant, Vassilios Kozmas, who uncovered huge losses, having tried to redo the books into a proper format. 'I alerted Simon and John and they cleaned out the team. I asked for three months to see if I could save the wiped-out investment.'

Nagle headed to London on a mission to find a copywriter to give P&G confidence and help pitch new business. 'Meandering around the creative department I was introduced to Ed Jones and convinced him to come to Jeddah to have a look. My intention was to kidnap him! Ed duly arrived and made an immediate impact on P&G. Meanwhile Vassilios was uncovering more financial mess, and we had about twelve weeks to make a go of it.' A pitch for Saudi American Bank in early December was the lucky break. (For Nagle's account of the unusual but necessary recruitment to make the pitch successful, see Chapter 2.)

If markets in the Middle East were underdeveloped, there were areas of Eastern Europe where these markets simply didn't exist. The fall of the Berlin Wall changed all that. Simon Goode was Saatchi & Saatchi's general manager EMEA (Europe, Middle East & Africa) at the time, and recollects how Saatchi & Saatchi were initially ahead of the game in Eastern Europe: 'Mike Parker did some early work out of London with Solidarity and Lech Wałęsa in around 1986 or 1987.

He did this with a couple of ex-pat entrepreneurial Polish brothers, Marek and Jan Jaroszewicz. Based in London, they had "contacts" on all sides of the political divide in Poland. The initial activity came and went, but when political changes started in Poland (and the rest of Eastern Europe), these brothers, with an eye for an opportunity, proposed we set up a joint venture agency with them. They'd provide the premises, and some local people with at least some degree of credible credentials in marketing under the state-controlled agencies (of which there were just two – one for import promotion and the other for export promotion).

'The joint venture was to be 50/50, which was not something Saatchis would go for normally, but in order to be one of the first western agencies in Eastern Europe we proposed to the plc [Saatchis' holding company] that we compromise. Think of the publicity, we said. They wanted to know how much capital was needed. Fifty thousand pounds, we said. We'd done our homework! One hundred thousand pounds start-up capital is nothing.' Unfortunately, it seems the usual Saatchi & Saatchi buccaneering, entrepreneurial spirit had gone missing that day. "No," they said. "Too risky. Who knows what the hell will happen in Eastern Europe?" This was in 1990. The Wall had only been down a few months.' Ultimately, it was an expensive lapse of Saatchi spirit.

'Saatchi & Saatchi plc still went with the Jaroszewicz brothers who were delighted to put up all the capital. We signed an Associate Agreement [not unlike a franchise] with them, where they paid a peanuts fee annually, and an option to buy at least 51 per cent, and we would spend no end of time trying to get their marketing/advertising "experts" to accept even the rudiments of how to look after our clients. Fast-forward just two years and someone in plc was reviewing the company's activities in developing markets, and felt that Eastern Europe would be the land of golden opportunity and said we should invest in Poland first as it was showing signs of becoming the most stable of the emergent ex-communist markets! We pointed out how we'd proposed this only a couple of years earlier and it had been dismissed. "Doesn't matter, we need to demonstrate to investors and clients we're ahead of the game."

'We then pointed out that, given the growth of the business and its potential now, and our reputation established as the most dynamic western agency brand, it wouldn't be cheap. "Yeah whatever!" came the response.

'Around nine months later, after hours and hours of hard negotiation with the Polish brothers and their lawyers, it cost Saatchi & Saatchi plc £1.5 million to buy the majority share of the agency. The Polish brothers were rather pleased with the return on their investment.

"The biggest risk is in not taking risks."

'I learned this at Saatchi & Saatchi, but the plc seldom let us live it. That said, worldwide CEO Robert Louis-Dreyfus was eventually very supportive about getting involved in Eastern Europe, once I'd presented a convincing strategy and a plan.'

Goode observes that this was not an isolated incident of (uncharacteristic) corporate timidity that resulted in missed opportunity: 'Mark King [see page 149] and I both remember the time when Saatchis' local supplier and potential trading partner in Russia, Video International, were in severe financial difficulties. They were desperate for a U-Matic video machine, worth a few hundred pounds. So desperate, in fact, they were willing to offer Saatchis a major share in the company in return for the machine. The go-ahead was not given. Video International turned into a multibillion-dollar media conglomerate.'

A Saatchi & Saatchi agency was also set up in Hungary, in 1990. Here was another market with no tradition of advertising to speak of, but Saatchis saw the potential. A Brit, William Leach (mentioned in Chapter 3) arrived in Budapest as the agency's first managing director, six weeks after Hungary's first free elections. 'We started the agency in the attic of a local's house. We took the doors off the two attic rooms and perched them on milk crates to make two desks. We hired a Hungarian-speaking art director from New York as our creative director, and away we went. We had P&G and British Airways as foundation clients. They billed about $500,000 (not income, billing). There was me, our CEO, Imre Kovats (a Hungarian national but a former intelligence officer in the Austrian army), our NY creative director, a multilingual, six-foot Amazon office manager, and a phone.

'The phone was significant. At that time there were few, if any offices available with a phone. If you saw a phone in an office for rent, it was rare that it had ever or would ever be connected. Formerly, the communist state only wanted phones in the hands of anarchists so they could monitor conversations. So the infrastructure was virtually non-existent (and there were no mobile phones).'

CEO Imre Kovats gets on with business in Saatchis' new 'office' in Hungary.

Imre Kovats elaborates: 'When three lines (one of which was used for the fax) became insufficient, dropping an envelope in the right place in the still state-owned telecom office with a petition in hard currency helped us get the fourth line. Then we convinced our neighbour to share his private phone with us during working hours in exchange for picking up his total phone bill. And finally, when we had to rent an additional office two miles away (in a purpose-built apartment block mysteriously converted for business use), once more with the help of a magic envelope, two miles of private phone cable were laid under the streets of Budapest.'

Before the phone issues were resolved, Leach explains how they coped: 'We had to rely on the written word [in 1991 email didn't exist of course]. We had a fleet of taxis waiting outside our building and if we wanted to get an urgent message to a client, we simply wrote it down and had a taxi driver deliver it. We worked amazingly hard – 100-hour weeks were not unusual. A Dunkirk spirit and regular parties ensured we maintained a brilliant culture, and impromptu meetings would occur wherever we met our clients – at pubs and clubs as well as conventional meeting rooms. Imre and I even dipped into our own bank accounts sometimes to pay our employees, but that again was the Saatchi spirit thriving.'

Nearby Yugoslavia, unlike other communist states, had a developed, more western-style economy. It also had an advertising industry and one of its leading figures was Ivan Stankovic. 'The story of Saatchis in the Balkans began in Belgrade, in the country then known as Yugoslavia, at 6.50 a.m. one morning in May 1990 when Simon Goode stopped over on his flight from Istanbul to London. We closed a deal very quickly, and by 8 a.m. we were celebrating our new affiliation with the local brandy, *slivovitz*, on a barge on the Danube. At the time, I was working in the leading Yugoslav agency and was having lots of disputes with my boss, Dragan Sakan (Saki, a true creative legend) and was seriously thinking about starting my own agency. Saatchi's proposal came at the right time and with some suggestions from mutual friends, I decided to offer Saki a partnership. Of course, he would be president, I vice president so everybody was happy. Someone more so than the other.'

Goode recalls, 'We weren't actually expecting to move into Yugoslavia quite so soon. But a chance meeting between international strategic planning director Mike Liebling and Sakan and Stankovic at the [Yugoslavian] Golden Drum Advertising Festival meant an earlier introduction to two bloody good people with impressive credentials sooner than we expected, so it was a no-brainer. I wasn't actually looking for other choices. Right people, right time.'

But before long, chaos arrived in Yugoslavia. In Stankovic's words, 'In 1991 the disintegration of Yugoslavia started and my country disappeared. I lost my country, my identity. Bloody wars became a painful reality and we were on the main news on every TV station.' When Slovenia became the first country to break away from Yugoslavia, Ivan and his colleagues began a regional operation establishing a new office in Slovenia at the beginning of 1992. The same year they opened up in Bulgaria, and then Croatia, Macedonia, Bosnia and Albania.

Stankovic gives a first-hand account of the conditions they had to work under at the time: 'Communications and travel were huge problems. There were no telephone lines between Belgrade and

Slovenia. Every kind of direct transport was cut off, and you were not allowed to enter Slovenia in a car with Serbian licence plates. I went back to my teenage and student days and rediscovered the bus. Travelling this distance (there's a motorway now and the 520 km journey takes about four and a half hours) became a new experience. The shortest trip took fifteen hours. The longest, one Christmas, took thirty hours. That one was a night drive, with the bus travelling through Hungary, where we changed from a Serbian bus on to a Slovenian one, with lots of customs inspections and suspicion.'

Imre Kovats, in Hungary, describes how he helped a Yugoslavian colleague whose mother was Serbian and his father Croatian. Each of these newly formed countries wanted him to serve in its army. 'We found a quick solution. We officially employed him in Saatchi Budapest, and he became a Hungarian resident, exempting him from military service in both countries.' His instant Hungarian was Ivan Stankovic. Some time later, Stankovic's business partner, Sakan, had to escape from Belgrade and he was smuggled at considerable personal expense and danger across the border to Hungary on the floor of a Mercedes.

Trying to run a business in Yugoslavia at all with rampant hyperinflation (2–3 per cent per hour) was an enormous challenge, and something Stankovic and Sakan's colleagues in Saatchi & Saatchi's European network would find hard to grasp. As Stankovic explains, 'We all became billionaires, as a single US dollar was worth, at one stage, 1,500 billion dinars.'

An economic disaster given a positive spin by Saatchi associates in Eastern Europe.

With Simon Goode's encouragement, Stankovic had some 10-billion-dinar notes mounted, as gifts for their European network colleagues. With the gift came a message from Stankovic and Sakan saying how they'd found an easier way to become billionaires. As Goode says, 'It worked. Everyone loved the gift, principally because of Ivan's and Saki's personalities.'

These two certainly 'got it'. Through being chairman of Saatchi & Saatchi's European Creative Board, Richard Myers developed a great personal friendship with Saki, and was very fond of this charismatic, generous, highly inventive and resourceful man from Belgrade.

Mark King was Saatchi & Saatchi's missionary to Russia, first in St Petersburg on an informal basis, supporting P&G as Agency of Record, and then formally in Moscow (combined with Bates). As King explains, his timing was not perfect when he volunteered to move out of the pricey Grand Hotel Europe to live more economically in a rented apartment amongst the townsfolk. It was the very day the tanks rolled into Moscow and St Petersburg to defend an attempt to depose President Yeltsin.

'Robert Fletcher (nominally overseeing our interests in Russia and other Eastern European markets from Saatchi's Frankfurt office) made a naive, if well-intentioned call to my wife back home in London to ask if she knew where I was at the time, because there was a military coup going on and I should get out fast. Being somewhat preoccupied at that particular moment with bringing up three small children, caring for a very sick parent and generally getting by with me in Russia for three-plus weeks a month, my wife pointed out to him in less than temperate language that the breaking political situation wasn't exactly top of her mind at that moment, but now he'd made her terrified about her husband's safety and since *he* had the resources of one of the world's largest ad networks at his disposal, why the fuck didn't he immediately face up to his duty of care as an employer, pull his finger out, locate me and call her when I'd been found!'

King also faced the fact that business couldn't be run by any normal western model in the beginning. 'As Saatchi didn't exist officially in Russia in my early months, there was no bank account and our only means of operating was via P&G alone (they thought

I was just working for them). Inflation was running at extremely high levels, the exchange rate was highly volatile. I was asked to buy a radio campaign in St Petersburg for a BBC World Service radio soap opera (nice irony for P&G, given their business) and payment worked like this: in London I went to the BBC's Bush House with an invoice for immediate settlement because the campaign needed to run asap. They remitted payment to Saatchi & Saatchi UK. The agency's accounts department gave me several thousand pounds' worth of US dollar travellers' cheques and I returned to Russia.

'I went to a bureau de change where I could get the best street rate outside of the Hotel (just across the road, fortunately) with the burliest chum I could find (an Irish film director) who wore his usual military greatcoat. I told him to stand close to me, looking as mean as a typical Russian bodyguard, with his hand tucked into his inner pocket as if holding a gun. We stood in the long queue of local street traders and mobsters converting their few dollars into roubles.

When it was my turn at the counter, the expectation of imminent mugging could be felt as I exchanged what, to locals, represented several lifetimes' earnings. We legged it back across the road to the relative safety of the hotel with, literally, sacks full of rouble banknotes. Later, under cover of darkness, I delivered the roubles to the local radio station and the campaign ran.'

The fate of a Saatchi & Saatchi financial director, who decided to check out the realities of doing business in Russia, before committing to opening a formal office, is also related by King: 'Munir Samji was somewhat sceptical that it was such a hostile environment for foreigners at that time. Of course, he's of Asian extraction, and racism was very evident then (and still is, to some extent). Bored, some underpaid police would also like to hassle foreigners to extract a bribe. I'd warned Munir, but I don't think he was quite prepared when our car from the airport into town was pulled over and he was given a particularly energetic shakedown by racist policemen when they saw who they had.'

The law was involved in another story from Russia – this time involving the tax police. Group account director Wouter Leydes remembers the day it happened: 'The day started as usual, as far as you could call any business day at the offices of Bates Saatchi & Saatchi Moscow usual. All of a sudden, the offices were invaded by some twenty men dressed in normal Russian clothing, some of them shouting orders in Russian; the entrance to the office was immediately sealed off by heavily armed, mean-looking Russians. It took a while before our Russian staff realized that it was a raid by the tax police (my Russian at the time was limited).

'We were not allowed to touch our computers, to answer the phone or to leave the room. To make sure we didn't, a surly looking man with a weapon on his hip took a chair and placed himself in the middle of my room. A senior officer walked into the room, and started to interview me. After a while, I realized he thought I was a kind of chief financial officer, because of the title on my business card: Group Account Director. I was lucky that, at the time, one of the account managers was a daughter of a Russian general and she made it very clear I wasn't the person they were looking for.

(Afterwards she explained that she had to use the authority of her father and her family name to convince them.)

'After this I started to realize that a lot of ex-pat colleagues were not in the office. Some were abroad, or just had a day off to show friends the beauty of Moscow. Our CEO was also abroad, and as I understand it, he believed that I too hadn't returned from my holiday. All the ex-pats were contacted and advised to leave the country as soon as possible because Bates Saatchi & Saatchi wanted to avoid the risk of our being captured and used as bargaining chips. For the first time I really started to feel very uncomfortable, particularly as I was one of the few ex-pats present in the building.

'As they were now convinced that I was not the CFO I was allowed to use my mobile phone again. I immediately called a Dutch friend, working at BBDO Moscow, and asked her to book a ticket to Amsterdam on my behalf. Because I didn't want the tax police to overhear me trying to flee the country, I asked her in Dutch "to buy a coupon for the big blue bird that could fly as soon as possible to our beautiful capital". I didn't dare use the words "KLM", "ticket", "Amsterdam" and "tonight"!

'A ticket was waiting for me at the KLM counter at the Sheremetyevo airport but I still had to get permission from the senior officer to leave the office. As I was recovering from a surgical incision, my knee was still taped up, and I had difficulty walking. So I explained that I really needed to go to my physiotherapy appointment and that I would return an hour and a half later. At first, permission was refused, but it was granted when I explained that I would leave everything on my desk – my laptop, office bag and so on. I could not use one of the dedicated office drivers because they were not allowed to leave the office. So I had to stop a "gypsy" taxi and asked him to drive to my apartment, wait for five minutes and then take me to the airport. Because it was rush hour he wasn't too keen to drive to the airport. But when I offered him $100 upfront, and another $100 if he got me to the airport in time to catch my flight, he was very keen, and was driving as if he was competing in the Monaco Grand Prix!

'One hour later I was in front of a customs officer at the airport. My heart rate was up 300 per cent. Thoughts were running through my mind that I could be stopped at the last moment (like in a bad movie), but when I heard the sound of my passport being stamped three times, I started to relax. My heart rate went back to normal the moment I set foot on the KLM flight. There I met Jeroen Peters, our creative director, who had been showing friends around Moscow that day. We got very drunk on board!'

Despite all the drama, the issue with the tax police was resolved in an entirely routine way. Saatchi & Saatchi paid a tax bill of $363,000, finally settled on 25 April 1997, according to the *Moscow Times*. However, this didn't stop a number of imaginative yet wholly wrong theories emerging about how the issue was resolved. Amongst these possibly vodka-fuelled flights of fancy was the one about certain Russian officials being offered the keys to Saatchi-owned villas in southern Spain. Total fiction.

Personal danger and discomfort are a missionary hazard, but it illustrates how important ingenuity and resilience have been for Saatchi people when they've been strangers in strange lands. Back in Saudi Arabia, when the struggling agency was just about turning the corner with P&G and Saudi American Bank as clients, 'All hell broke loose,' recalls Gerry Nagle. 'The coalition forces started bombing Iraq. Ed Jones and I shared an apartment in an ex-pat compound, Arabian Homes, in Jeddah, and the day the war started we drove to the airport to take a sightseer's look at all the B52 bombers there. Our house was stocked with war rations and our escape route was with P&G. Their general manager put together an excellent emergency plan, with a boat in Jeddah to escape in case it got too hot!'

Stephen Hahn-Griffiths, strategic planning director of Saatchi & Saatchi Budapest, describes how his office won a major multi-national Agency of Record assignment for Mars across Eastern Europe. 'With a mandate to launch Mars into Romania, Bulgaria, even war-ravaged Croatia, Serbia, and beyond, I set off on a wing and a prayer with a British passport in hand and a fist full of dollars. Intent on bringing the first consumer packaged-goods brand to market, I encountered some excruciatingly difficult, and occasionally dangerous travel experiences, communist-style interrogations and mountains of red tape to secure the opportunity to launch Snickers, Milky Way and M&Ms etc. on state-run TV networks across the region.

'On one trip, I arrived in Albania to be greeted by a traffic jam of cows clogging the Tirana airport exit road. I took the only option and hired a horse and carriage to take me to my meeting. Later that day, I was invited to dinner to meet some prominent government and business dignitaries at Tirana's "best" restaurant.

'There was a particularly awkward moment when I was presented to a scary-looking former Miss Albania, who immediately saw me as a potential suitor, and possible one-way ticket out of Tirana! Anxious to make a graceful exit, I left to check into a dilapidated hotel, only to find my reservation was not valid. Now it was close to midnight and I was thankful to be offered the sanctuary of being able to sleep on the floor at the British Consulate.'

Danger, and the key antidotes, quick thinking and resourcefulness, were recurring themes across the Saatchi & Saatchi network. Pete Watkins was the regional CEO in Asia: 'The agency in Jakarta had been a perennial problem. When I arrived in 1992 we conducted an investigation into corruption and kickbacks. Stuff always seemed to be going on, and despite every effort and investment (money, time, people), we were unable to make a go of it, despite having clients like P&G and HP. On top of that there were occasional riots, and one time I flew the CEO and his family out for safety. In the end I had had enough.

'The big problem at the time was that foreign entities had no legal standing in Indonesia. You were there by the grace of your joint-venture partner – normally some obscure member of the ruling elite/ royalty. They wanted the prestige of an international relationship. Only one foreign company, IBM, had ever tried to win legal redress and they'd lost. Put simply, everything was in the joint-venture partner's name – they owned the company, the building, the land. They signed for everything, had the banking, etc. However, we paid for everything. And the agency lost money hand over fist. In a moment of desperation, I sat down with our Asia finance director and asked a simple question: if we close it and walk away, what are the liabilities? The answer was simple, too: nothing – because our name isn't on anything. The up side was we would stop losing money.

'I arranged for the multinational clients to be handled by our sister agency Bates for a percentage. I conducted a review and the local representatives and JV partner made the case for improvements and for Saatchi & Saatchi to stay in Indonesia. I had not informed them that I had already made a decision, but at the end of the meeting I told them. They were askance. What were they to do without big clients? They had employees. They had a building. Debts, bank loans, all manner of problems. I informed them of the local law, i.e. it wasn't my problem, and I left.

'But here is my problem. I have basically given a member of the local royalty a slap in the face. I'm on my own in Jakarta. The cab takes a different, new-to-me route to the airport and I begin to think, "Where are we going?"

'And perhaps, "What's going to happen to me?" I sweated it all the way, looking for any clue, any geographical landmark I could recognize. It was the longest cab ride of my life as I seriously considered the possibility I would be "hit".

'Finally we popped out of nowhere right by the airport. However, for the entire time I was in the airport waiting for my flight, I jumped every time a passenger's name was called. Then there was a short delay to the flight, for no reason. "They're not going to let me out," I thought. But all's well that ends well, and perhaps nothing was ever going to happen. But I have never been to Indonesia again. Not even to Bali.'

Pete Watkins isn't the only Saatchi & Saatchi employee to find himself in an uncomfortable position. When Graham Thomas was CEO of Saatchi & Saatchi's Tokyo office, he was arrested as he led a demonstration arranged by the agency for the charity Jubilee 2000. This coincided with the G8 summit in Japan, targeted by the charity to campaign for debt relief for the world's poorest countries. Thomas was seen arguing with the police and the next minute he was being hauled off to one of the waiting vans. The BBC came to his rescue, and after about fifteen minutes of their reporter acting as an intermediary, Thomas was back on the march, as belligerent as ever.

Although acquisitions played a major role in Saatchi & Saatchi's growth and ultimately, the number-one spot worldwide, they weren't all seen as economically sound. For example, the purchase of Bates for $450 million in 1986 was seen by some people as just an expensive, reckless pursuit of the top spot. But Simon Mellor, who was deeply involved in the deal as director of Saatchi & Saatchi plc, has a different take on it: 'Back then, one part of the strategy was to build a company with two networks (now WPP have four, Omnicom three, so maybe not so stupid!). We had discussions with DDB and BBDO, two major global agency networks. Neither came to anything because of very significant conflicts, particularly with P&G. Bates had a fantastic international network – number one in each Scandinavian market, in Australia, other parts of Europe and big, if dull, in the US. (They also owned an agency in Minneapolis that was bigger and more profitable than any agency in the UK.) So, in one sense, a logical deal to do. The City was also very keen on it at the time. There was always pressure from the City to keep growing.

BAT£S

'It was a lot of money, but then Bates made a lot of money, so the multiple wasn't outrageous. I think it was a lower multiple than WPP paid for major global agency networks JWT or Ogilvy (though clearly not such a good business). In a way it was a bit like buying a public company where you have to pay all (or in Bates' case most) of the money up front to people who aren't necessarily the most deserving.

'Unfortunately, the ownership structure meant that a very few people got an awful lot of money – and Bob Jacoby, who was the CEO, had a "golden share" which meant he got an even more disproportionate share of the whole. I don't think that legally we could do anything about that (other than walk away). The other factor was that there weren't any other viable networks to buy, and Bates knew that.

'People ask, how come we didn't foresee the massive loss of clients that followed? Well, I spent over a year meeting with John Hoyne who was Bates' head of international and number two or three in their business, going through all the clients of all their offices around the world, trying to identify potential conflicts. We looked at every client, in every agency in every country and came up with a list of potential client losses.

'There were some which were obvious, such as direct P&G conflicts (and P&G were much tougher on conflict back then), to possibles such as car clients, to some really obscure ones, but we tried to quantify them all and the possible impact on the businesses. The two networks were not being merged in any way, so we were also hopeful that some of those clients identified would not have a problem being in a network that was itself owned by a group within which there were conflicts.

'In the event, some of the clients we had identified left, but a whole number of others took the opportunity of the deal to leave. This was particularly true of some global clients headquartered in the US. Conflict was not the reason. I think they just hated Bates and had had enough of them.'

The high pace of growth through multiple acquisitions led to some interesting questions. Sally De Rose, in her role as head of business information, remembers being asked by someone from Charles and Maurice's office, some time after Saatchis had bought the Compton network, 'Could you tell me where Compton have offices exactly?'

With the empire built, there have been numerous formal efforts to spread the Saatchi word, some with considerable success. For example, a reportedly 'difficult' meeting Warman and Bannister had with senior DFS executives in New York (see page 138) was followed by a dinner with the pair of them and around eight less senior agency employees. Account director Suzanne Douglas was given the role of host. 'Before I left for the dinner, Beau Fraser, head of new business, said, "Suzanne, make absolutely sure that the wine keeps flowing all night. Do not hesitate. Just order and keep ordering." I did as I was told. About two hours in, Beau arrived to join the dinner. Sitting on the table was a lone bottle of red wine, about one third full. Beau was furious. "I thought I told you to keep the wine flowing," he hissed under his breath. "I did," I replied. "That's our twenty-first bottle."'

There was a feeling at one time that of all the markets in the Saatchi & Saatchi empire, the US was the one that 'didn't get it'. To help overcome this, Simon Goode proposed, and then ran, a programme of junior creative team exchanges between London and New York. According to Goode, teams from both sides of the Atlantic 'had terrific times and experiences'. Norm Magnusson, with his creative partner Stink Miller, came over to Saatchis London and said,

'For a couple of young creatives, getting paid in what was then the almighty American dollar, London was the centre of a beautiful and unknown universe and we explored as much as we could. If the "small Saatchi world" initiative's goal was to create a stronger, more cohesive and communicative corporate culture, I really couldn't say how well it accomplished this goal. If, however, it was to send a bunch of young creatives on the adventure of their lives and to help them create friendships across the pond that would last forever, it was a roaring, drunken success.'

Cultural differences will always be a minefield for global companies. It's one thing to negotiate this hazard when it's between offices within the network, but inevitably, global expansion brings potential clashes with clients and local populations. Sometimes offence can be caused accidentally, carelessly, unintentionally, or by sheer unforeseen bad timing.

The latter two applied in 1998, when Australia held a Constitutional Convention to discuss whether Australia should become a republic. At the time, almost all opinion polls suggested a clear majority in favour of a republic.

So Saatchi's Sydney office ran a full-page ad with the headline:

'DON'T WORRY YOUR MAJESTY, YOU'RE NOT THE ONLY BRITISH EXPORT THAT'S HAD ITS DAY.'

Beneath it was a picture of the front of a battered Range Rover, and beneath that a Lexus logo (the luxury Toyota brand).

As Mike Satterthwaite, then CFO of the Sydney agency, recalls, 'We expected some complaints from ardent Australian royalists and resident Poms.' But on the other side of the world, bad timing reared its ugly head and, stoked by Fleet Street indignation, created a rather more serious outcome. 'Within a day of the ad appearing, a copy of it was printed on the front page of the UK's *Daily Telegraph* with the headline **"TOYOTA ADVERT INSULTS QUEEN"**. Unfortunately, the ad appeared when Emperor Akihito's state visit to the UK was imminent.

'The Japanese were embarrassed. The emperor wasn't happy and someone would have to pay for this – most likely the agency. But we were saved by our CEO, Brian Sheehan. He'd previously been CEO of Saatchi & Saatchi Tokyo so he knew exactly how to apologize the Japanese way.'

A little closer to careless is the Dunlop trade campaign, launching the new fuel-saving Denovo tyre in the UK, during the first oil crisis. Created by Saatchis London, the ad featured a cartoon Arab, complete with a big hooked nose, red-checked headgear, and holding a curved dagger in a threatening manner. The headline went something like, 'DON'T BE BLACKMAILED BY...'. The media executive on the business, Peter Setterington, tells the story: 'This campaign was about to break in virtually every trade paper that had anything to do with cars. In other words, lots. And just as the first magazines were about to hit the news stands, Tim Bell got a call from the Foreign Office saying the campaign had to be stopped. Somehow, the ad had been seen by someone in the Saudi Arabian embassy – and the threat was to cancel every single order their country had with the UK, unless the campaign was pulled. Hundreds of millions of pounds in exports were at risk.

'I was called down to Tim's office and he asked if we could cancel. "No way," I said. "Some of the magazines are already in the distribution chain – they've all gone to press. We're talking hundreds of thousands of copies!"' Setterington witnessed a three-way crisis phone conversation between Bell, the MD of Dunlop and the head of the Foreign Office, which reached the conclusion that the campaign just had to be stopped. But the hard question was, how? Setterington believes he came up with the only way to do it. Buy every single copy of every single magazine. And he was given this near impossible job himself. 'I managed to buy the entire circulation of half a dozen magazines and had the ad cut from every single copy of half a dozen others, at a considerable discount.'

When Setterington explained the situation and the possible consequences, the publications had been very understanding. 'Not a single copy of the ad saw the light of day and hundreds of millions of pounds' worth of British exports were saved.'

There has also certainly been the odd occasion where Saatchi people have been very much innocents abroad. On a fact-finding mission to Japan, ahead of a major campaign about the relaunch of Datsun as Nissan, a talented art director, Mike Shaffron, was heard

to ask one of the Japanese hosts of the Saatchi team, 'Don't you get bored with Japanese food?' In a similar vein, but not confirmed, Shaffron, seeing the minimalism in a client's home, allegedly asked, very sympathetically, 'Oh dear! What happened to the rest of your furniture?'

Some redemption for Shaffron came with his award-winning TV commercial, which broke new ground by not talking about car models at all, but instead compared Nissan's work ethic with the status quo of poor quality, industrial strife and aloof management common in UK factories at the time.

By contrast, however, the account director leading that trip to Japan, Simon De Mille, had his cultural antennae fully working. 'I'd spent some time, prior to the campaign running, selling the idea inside Nissan HQ in Tokyo. I'd made three trips without success. I hadn't realized, at first, their system for checking out suppliers was to test the commitment of the individual as much as the company. I was asked by [regional CEO] Roderick More if I would consider becoming Saatchi & Saatchi's man in Tokyo to combine the Nissan business with others in the growing roster (including British Airways). I took my wife and, at the time, very blonde four-year-old daughter. Once the export general manager of Nissan met her at dinner and taught her how to use chopsticks the business was won. It was the commitment they wanted to see. In the end, I didn't go to Japan – it wasn't right for my family.'

A similar outbreak of cultural sensitivity was demonstrated by strategic planner Bob Roscow. A joint venture was set up between RCA

and Hitachi to launch a 'video-disc-player', a forerunner of DVDs and DVD players.

The joint venture was headed by an American, and Saatchi's launch script had been approved in the successful pitch for the business. Two weeks later, Roscow was unexpectedly called upon to describe the planned TV campaign to a very senior executive from Hitachi headquarters in Japan.

The core of the idea for the TV commercial was a deserted Trafalgar Square in London on New Year's Eve when, normally, the Square would be absolutely heaving with revellers. But this time, everybody was at home enjoying the new Hitachi invention. The statue of the victorious British naval hero, Lord Nelson, the centrepiece of the square, comes to life, wonders where everyone is, and discovers the invention for himself.

Roscow elaborates a little. 'Received wisdom, back in 1983 or so, was that Japanese clients were a little sensitive about any mention of the Second World War, and, by extension, any war. They didn't approve of statues of military heroes. Plus, they are big on respect and dignity. If there were a revered figure to whose memory a statue had been erected, then that figure would be treated with honour and respect. You wouldn't abuse their memory by dragging them into a sales message. You certainly wouldn't animate them for your purpose.'

Roscow also noted that the important visitor was probably between sixty and sixty-five years old, making him in his early twenties during the Second World War. He

realized just how dangerous most of the script was. Not mentioning war was the easy bit. In an astonishing display of the verbal equivalent of Fred Astaire footwork, Roscow succeeded. The commercial was made and ran as scripted.

There's a category of intercultural mishaps that are best described as 'Oops! No harm done.' Peter Cullinane was worldwide COO and he spills the beans on a couple of lapses: 'My worst diplomatic performance was when visiting Saudi Arabian multibillionaire, Prince Al-Waleed bin Talal bin Abdul Aziz al-Saud, who, at the time, was a major Saatchi & Saatchi shareholder.

'I was determined not to repeat [Saatchi & Saatchi chairman] Bob Seelert's faux pas which saw him, having spent the flight over from New York rehearsing how he should greet the Saudi royal, put it all prematurely to effect when he mistook the driver, who met him at the plane's door, for the prince and proceeded to scrape and bow to the bemused driver. I didn't make the same mistake and made it uneventfully to the palace where I waited for several hours in the presence of an urbane and immaculately dressed assistant in his dazzlingly white thawb. Desperate to find something interesting to say, I finally decided to draw on my P&G experience and asked him how he got his clothes so white. Needless to say, he had no idea, and thought the question so outlandish that I think he consigned me to the idiot box.'

Unsurprisingly there have been times in Saatchis' history when 'foreigners' have pushed back. As his name suggests, the one-time CEO of Saatchi & Saatchi Germany, Hubertus von Lobenstein, is aristocratic. He recalls two encounters with worldwide CEO Kevin Roberts. The first, soon after Roberts was appointed in 1997, was at a regional conference in Istanbul: 'During breaks in the main programme, a number of one-on-one meetings were scheduled with Kevin. Finally it was Hun time. So I started to introduce ourselves, the agency, our challenges and so on. A couple of minutes in, I realized Kevin wasn't listening. He just stared at me. Finally, he interrupted my short, witty, well-rehearsed presentation.

Kevin:	Who do you think you are?
Me:	??
Kevin:	Your language!
Me:	???
Kevin:	Your English is British English!
Me:	?????
Kevin:	I don't like it! Don't speak like that! I've got enough of those bastards around me. From now on, you either speak English with a German accent, or American English. No snob language! Clear? Now start again!'

Later, when Roberts paid his first official visit to the Frankfurt office, von Lobenstein was determined to make it 'very memorable'. 'We told him to bring his sports gear (we knew he was a sports fanatic) and picked him up at his hotel at 7.30 a.m. We, meaning the board and two employees who happened to be members of the bronze-medal-winning German 4 x 400m relay team from the 1988 Seoul Olympics. When Kevin realized who he was running with, competition set in. The result after one hour of exercise? The CEO, lying on his back in the agency's reception, with two lovely receptionists massaging their worldwide boss's aching calves.

'One lunch later with our hottest and youngest talent, and one dinner later on a go-cart track, and the verdict on the Huns was reached. Kevin's executive assistant in New York, Trudy Vitti, reported to them, "Kevin just came back. I don't know what you've done with him, but he thinks you Germans are totally crazy."'

Saatchi & Saatchi had a relationship with an agency in Japan called Yomiko. It was run by Kuroki-san, who was, according to Pete Watkins, 'Smart and always interested in having fun with westerners and learning a little about them in the process.' But Watkins went along to their first meeting not knowing this. 'He carefully looked me up and down. He paused and then asked me why I looked like a game-show host.'

'What's the problem with eating whales?'

On another occasion, they went out to lunch and Watkins deferred to his host, allowing him to order the food. 'The food arrives and Kuroki-san offers me the whale bacon. Now what do I do? Immediately I thought, this is probably the only chance I'll ever get to eat whale and after all, it's already dead and on the plate. He asked me what I thought of it and the conversation moved on.

'Then from nowhere, he asked, "What's the problem with eating whales?" Again, thrown by Kuroki-san's mischievousness, I came up with a shameful answer. "I don't know. I've never seen a dinosaur, would it matter if my children never saw a whale?" At this point, Saatchi & Saatchi Japan's CEO, Brian Sheehan, nearly choked.'

Copywriter Rod Lyons notes that there were odd consequences to winning the Conservative Party account, one of which being that political parties around the world seemed to think they needed the magic Saatchi touch to make them successful. One of these was a political party in Nigeria, allegedly one of the most corrupt places on earth at the time. 'The charming account director Roderick More was handed the assignment. When he arrived in Lagos with our creative work, a couple of local problems arose: the customs officer told More that his gold Parker pen was an absolutely banned item in Nigeria and immediately confiscated it. Stepping out of customs, pen-less, More was met by a man who said he had been sent to take care of a prized guest to his country and would assist in changing currency while he waited. Yes, you've got it. That was the last More saw of him. It's said that the agency fee arrived via a shipping company in London's Mile End Road in bank notes thought to have been appropriated from Nigeria's Hospital Development Fund.' Sally De Rose remembers, 'We asked for payment up front, a lot, and the next day a sack of dollar bills was delivered to our reception.'

ZZZZZZZZZZZZZZZZZZZZZZZZZ

The designer Nick Darke recalls working on the packaging for a range of French salad dressings being launched in the UK by Lesieur Alimentaire. Darke and Pete Watkins travelled to Paris the day before the presentation of the designs. After a heavy night on the town with the clients, Darke says that the next morning, with no time for breakfast and feeling dreadful, 'we set off in a taxi for the meeting…after the usual greetings, we all sit down around a big boardroom table and I begin to present the work. In no time at all, I hear snoring. Watkins is fast asleep. I make a move to wake him, but the senior client stops me. "Non, non. Leave him. He obviously needs the sleep." I finish my presentation, during which the snoring volume has been gradually increasing. The client then taps Watkins on the shoulder and says, "Wake up, Peter, you can go home now." '

Pete Watkins himself describes having difficulties with Salomon, the French winter sports company. 'I do recall a reconciliation of sorts with the senior client, Gilles Descampes. He leant over to me at dinner and, in a moment of great candour and honesty, said, "You know, Pete, the problem with you English is that you are as arrogant as we French are." '

Arguably it is possible to identify the moment when the Saatchis global network really began to work. When Linda Locke was MD and executive creative director of Saatchi & Saatchi Singapore, she felt that too much of the network's creative image was focused on London, 'So I approached the London office about publishing a creative book. Not any old creative book but one based on "the best of the best". All work from around the world that had previously won awards would be eligible to then be judged by a group of creative peers at Saatchis. Jeremy Sinclair agreed. We got to some fabulous work for

The Best of the Best, front cover: Ralph Steadman's take on the Pregnant Man.

British Airways when Jeremy, who had been very quiet through the bulk of the judging, let out a sigh.

"At last they understand the tone."

'When we asked him what he meant, he explained that sometimes it was the tone of voice of the brand that gave it distinction. I never forgot this insight.' Their collaboration over this book was a defining moment for the global network: united by the pursuit of creative excellence, and sharing inspirational highlights and outstanding ideas between offices around the world.

Certainly, being able to pull off 'The World's Biggest Offer' for British Airways, as described in Chapter 6, indicated that Saatchi & Saatchi's global network had great cohesion, and an ability to rise to the most complex and challenging projects. But it's Richard Myers's view that Bob Isherwood, who took over as worldwide creative director soon after Charles and Maurice left the company, partnering Kevin Roberts, was responsible for developing a strategy that helped create an inclusive, ambitious and mutually supportive global network.

Under Isherwood's chairmanship, the Worldwide Creative Board was highly influential in setting the company's course. The board maximized the global reach of the network to source the content for some truly memorable Saatchi & Saatchi New Directors' Showcases at the Cannes International Advertising Festival, now the Cannes Festival of Creativity. (The Showcase had been devised, incidentally, in 1991 by the late Jim Baker, then head of TV in Charlotte Street.) Isherwood drove the network to be highly successful creatively. It punched way above its weight, in terms of number of offices and employees, and in 2002 Saatchi & Saatchi won more Cannes Lions than any other network ever. Bob Isherwood was definitely a man with a mission, accomplished.

Chapter 9

'SOMETIMES, MAURICE, I CAN'T BELIEVE WE CAME FROM THE SAME WOMB!'

Saatchi & Saatchi is a family business. Of course, only the two founding brothers are biologically connected, but they're responsible for a unique corporate DNA that sprang directly from their very particular way of thinking and acting.

THE SAATCHI BROTHERS' belief that they could achieve anything, that there were no boundaries, and that there were no rules that particularly mattered, was present from the beginning, and later expressed as 'nothing is impossible'. Similarly, the tenet articulated by Jeremy Sinclair as 'it's good to be big, it's better to be good, but it's best to be both' had been evident well before the brothers set up the company.

Both Charles and Maurice were ambitious. Both had a taste for good quality. In Charles's case this was obvious in his single-minded pursuit of creative originality and excellence and, in a more mundane sense, in his love of exclusive cars. When he was still a young copywriter at CDP, he asked for a company loan so he could buy a house. The loan was granted and Charles promptly bought a Ferrari. (Someone commented that with his looks and that car he didn't need a house – he'd always have a bed for the night.)

When account handler Sean O'Connor joined Saatchi & Saatchi, the company was still very young, but its mythology was already rich and plentiful. A popular story about the early days of the agency was that Charles had once got the keys from an estate agent to view some offices and had then had the locks changed and moved a chunk of the agency in. Another story suggested that Charles kept his Rolls-Royce 'new' by replacing the number plates with updated ones.

O'Connor's summary of the company's character goes like this: 'The agency culture was very tight and had the attitude of the mongrel fighter, a kind of "we may be brash outsiders but we're going to win" certainty. The strategy was based on daring and speed, not preciousness and self-regard.' He adds that even by the time he joined, 'the cult of the agency was already laid down, naughty and fearless, and anyone who wasn't prepared to add to this legend was made to feel very much at sea'.

Adam Crozier describes the culture as 'complicated yet clear' and largely creative-led, and attributes a lot of the agency's success to 'its ability to grapple with big company complexities and break them down to simple heart-of-the-matter nuggets'. His key word for the culture of Saatchi & Saatchi is courage.

Another word that encapsulates the Saatchi & Saatchi attitude established by Charles and Maurice is passion. Charles and

Maurice's robust exchanges of view are legendary. They are passion in action. According to the brothers' one-time PA, Nick Crean, 'There was a marvellous newspaper cartoon showing Maurice's office having been trashed by Charles. I saw it happen for real a few times. Huge brotherly anger and shouting and the crash of Maurice's massive white desk being turned upside down, coffee flying and anything and everything hurtled to the floor.' At the conclusion of these events, Crean says, 'Charles always stormed off home. Maurice's head would inevitably appear, slightly flushed, around the door asking, "Perhaps someone could get a dustpan and brush?"' Stephen Fox, account handler, remembers 'Two occasions in Lower Regent Street discussing the "problems of noisy decorators" with Unipart and with Dunlop clients, while chairs were being flamboyantly rearranged in Charles's office next door'.

Typographer Dave Wood was caught in the crossfire of an outbreak of brotherly difference of opinion. 'It was about 8 a.m. I was putting together an artwork for a press ad for Charles ahead of a 10 o'clock client meeting. These were pre-Mac days and artworks were created by manually "pasting" paper type and images onto a mounting board, which was held in place on a drawing board with masking tape. The artwork was virtually complete when Charles came in. As was often the case, he made a few changes. I'd just finished these, after carefully lifting the prints, re-gluing, trimming and repositioning as Charles has requested, when the (self-closing) door sprang open again and in walked Maurice. After a couple of pleasantries he looked over my shoulder at the ad and was perplexed, because the ad was now rather different from the layout we had agreed the previous evening. I explained about Charles having already been in. Maurice quietly asked me to ignore Charles and with a parting, "Back as it was, please – I'll talk to Charles," he walked out of the studio.

'After ten minutes I'd tediously revised the artwork back again when in walked Charles to review "his" work. He saw the ad and asked what the fuck I'd been doing. When I explained Maurice's intervention he was very unhappy. Now, rather loudly, he asked me to return the ad to *his* version and stormed out.

'So, for the second time, up came all the prints, carefully lifted, re-glued and repositioned. The door opened. In walked Maurice who was just as irked to see the ad still wasn't looking as he'd asked. As I began to explain, the door opened again and (thankfully) in walked Charles.'

The inevitable exchange followed, culminating in Maurice, escaping with the artwork, hotly pursued by Charles. The row continued outside the self-closing door for a few seconds. Suddenly the door burst open and in flew Maurice, very fast, backwards, glasses askew and, more importantly, without the artwork, and fell to the floor by the side of Wood's desk. He calmly got up and walked out.

Charles wasn't averse to making fun of Maurice. Strategic planner Mike Liebling recalls meeting Charles with his dog in the lift, soon after Saatchi & Saatchi had moved into the Garland-Compton offices in Charlotte Street.

'I introduced myself and he introduced himself. He then pointed down to his dog. "You've met my brother, Maurice?"'

Charles came up with some classic lines aimed at Maurice. Mike Parker remembers Charles once saying, 'You fuckwit, Maurice, you're using your brains again.' And one-time PA to Charles and Maurice, Andrew Green, remembers a phrase worthy of inclusion as a Malcolm Tucker line in *The Thick Of It*: 'Why don't you *fuck off*, Maurice, and *stay fucked off.'*

On the wall behind Charles were three empty glass shelves on brackets, except one end of the middle shelf had slipped down and was resting on the bottom shelf.' Len Barkey recalls, visiting Charles in his office with some Health Education Council ads. '"One of those shelves is about to fall," I said. Charles looked at me pityingly. "It's a fucking picture," he said.'

Barkey also witnessed Charles's somewhat enhanced competitiveness. 'Charles and Maurice were very keen on tennis and played at an indoor club in Shepherds Bush. I played doubles with them on several occasions there. One day I invited them to the All England Club at Wimbledon to play on the grass with a fellow member, a New Zealand Davis Cup player, John McDonald. At the last minute Maurice had to cry off, so Mike Parker – a good player – stood in for him. McDonald partnered Charles, I partnered Parker. Unfortunately, Charles had a bad day, but McDonald was a good enough player to prevent Parker and me from winning too easily. In the locker room afterwards, I commiserated with Charles on the grounds that it was probably his first time playing on grass. "Never mind that," he said. "It's the first time I've ever fucking played outdoors!"'

Apparently, according to both (copywriters) Peter Wallach and David Bourne, Charles's need to win extended to Monopoly (played after work in the early days in Golden Square). 'If you'd bought Park Lane, say, and Charles wanted Park Lane, he would offer, in the spirit of benevolence, to take it off your hands. Decline the offer and Charles would increase his bid. If you were brave enough to still resist, Charles would double, even treble his offer. Refuse again, and having zapped you with the Saatchi death stare, he'd take out his wallet and in all seriousness and straight-facedly say, "Fuck you, here's £50 in real money for it!"'

All good creatives are passionate about their work and feel as protective about their ideas as they might towards their children. There's also a tradition of animosity and suspicion between creatives and account handlers. At Saatchis it wasn't unusual for differences of opinion between creatives and account handlers to progress from relatively calm debate to heated Anglo-Saxon exchanges and occasionally through to physicality.

As an example, account handler Jeremy Warshaw witnessed one particular confrontation between a highly talented creative and an account director who was well known for bravely (or foolishly) telling creative people what was wrong with their ideas. The heated Anglo-Saxon stage had been reached and it went something like this:

Creative:	Who are you calling a cunt?
Account director:	You.
Creative:	So you think I'm a cunt, do you?
Account director:	Yes, you're a cunt.

Naturally, stage three – physicality – followed fairly rapidly. At his desk outside the account director's office, Warshaw heard 'an almighty punch-up take place. I heard thuds, heavy breathing, furniture being thrown around and the obvious and unmistakable sound of wrestling. After about a minute of this, it went quiet.' What followed was a little unexpected. 'I heard guffaws of laughter. And after another few seconds they came out with their arms around each other and the last I heard as they left was them working out which restaurant they should go to for lunch.'

Warshaw also recalls how he had failed to sell an advertisement to a client and now as a consequence, he was being lifted by his lapels at least three inches off the ground by a creative group head responsible for the ad, giving Warshaw the benefit of an impromptu, yet memorable tutorial on the art of selling and on the precise nature of his role in the selling process.

Mark King soon discovered that a fighting spirit was also to be found in the company's Madison Avenue, New York, offices when he was seconded there from London between 1982 and 1984. 'A big and highly irascible guy was in charge of the flagship P&G account. By contrast, John LaPick was a refined, calm, greying creative director who wore bow ties, and worked on key parts of the business including the key Tide account, which was then in bad trouble.

'I had arrived from London, days before, to start as account director. The agency is suddenly put on formal notice by P&G [in other words, there was a threat that the account would be taken away from the agency unless certain improvements were made]. Cue panic, recriminations, prospect of sackings and disappearing bonuses! There ensued several awful moments that hit new lows in Saatchi creative standards, in interpersonal behaviour and in client-agency relations. But to my mind, the lowest point was when the big irascible guy was shouting at me in a corridor, insisting on me achieving some unrealistic production deadline he'd committed the agency to on one of my critical assignments (the launch of Tide Liquid).

'Mild-mannered John happens to pass by, starts defending me by explaining again to the irascible one why a production schedule was taking the time it did, and in seconds the two became embroiled in a wrestling match on the floor for all to see. An unedifying spectacle, to say the least. That very civilized mensch, Ed Wax (later chairman and CEO of Saatchi & Saatchi Worldwide) apologized to me and to John. The Tide business, by the way, was duly saved.'

Parties and fights can go hand in hand, although these may be less of the genuine punch-up type and more to do with misguided expressions of testosterone. John Honsinger describes a rather farcical example after a Christmas party in 1982. 'We had returned from our Christmas lunch held the day prior to breaking for the holidays. I was in my office and there was more noise and commotion than normal in our reception area so I went out to investigate. My creative director, Rick Smith, standing at five feet seven inches, was wrestling with Roy Warman, standing at six feet one inch at least, joint MD of Saatchi & Saatchi, chairman of my company, The Sales Promotion Agency, and a karate black belt.'

According to Rick Smith, 'We had all been drinking to huge excess of course, and were carrying on drinking in our reception area. I can't remember how the conversation started, but it ended up with Roy betting me I couldn't knock him over. I'm ashamed to say this led to Roy and me stripping down to our underpants. I decided the best way to knock Roy over was to launch myself at him from atop the reception desk, a task made more difficult because Peter Crossing was enjoying spraying said desk with lighter fuel and igniting it. Whilst I was leaping at Roy we managed to knock over the Christmas tree, scattering tinsel, twigs and baubles everywhere.'

Honsinger says, 'Trying to act responsibly, I attempted to intervene but then found myself being held around the throat and encouraged into a mock karate fight. With Rick's help I managed to wrestle Roy to the ground and with my arm around his neck, I again asked him to stop messing about. He responded by standing up, placing his foot in my stomach and throwing me to the other side of the room whilst still holding me. We landed with an unpleasant sickening thump. Roy ventured to ask if the noise was his arm breaking but I, holding my hand to my head, indicated otherwise. An ambulance was called. I was taken to hospital and required stitches to a gash above my eye.' (The injury was sustained, according to Smith, when Honsinger's head collided with the edge of a coffee table.)

Meanwhile, as Smith explains, 'Roy and myself, still in our underpants, sat and drank more beer in reception with a number of other staff who were also somewhat the worse for alcohol. At this point John's sister walked into reception (having just arrived from Canada) and was confronted by the appalling mess of a Christmas tree and decorations scattered over the floor, upturned furniture, a smoking reception desk and two grown men drinking beer in their underpants. John's sister, unfamiliar with the excesses of the ad industry, asked meekly, "I'm looking for John Honsinger?" to which we replied, "He's in hospital."'

According to Honsinger his sister did the decent thing and helped remove pine needles from Warman's backside. Peter Crossing (the casual arsonist mentioned earlier) was scarred in a different way. 'Roy's briefs were disgustingly skimpy and that image against Roy's ghostly white skin has remained with me for the rest of my life.'

There was a happy ending for John Honsinger. 'Four hours later I was out of hospital and round at The Carpenters Arms. I was greeted as a hero and received several proposals from pretty young girls. This was not an untypical happening at Saatchis.' When asked if this story is true, Roy Warman said, 'It could have taken place, I can't remember, but it was all part and parcel of the high jinx we all got up to at the time. Remember, throughout all this we were growing phenomenally, making money, creating great, award-winning work, doing winning media and helping our clients be massively successful.' Passion has certainly been poured into Saatchi & Saatchi celebrations as much as it has been poured into the work. It's reasonable to argue that Saatchi & Saatchi set the standard for lavishness and for the art of excess practised to perfection.

3,000 bottles of Lanson champagne were consumed at one of Saatchis' annual parties.

Agency parties in London were legendary. The day after one such party, strategic planning director Sue Moss remembers waking, a little blearily, to the news on the hugely popular Capital Radio that the agency had consumed 3,000 bottles of champagne. Art director, now photographer Alan Burles, captured some of the evidence. 'Work hard, play hard' has been something of an underassessment.

Responsible for putting together some of Saatchi & Saatchi's spectacular parties was travel and events manager Lyn Snudden (formerly Coade). For her first, she hired an empty warehouse in London's Docklands and installed a complete funfair. Seven hundred guests were transported there by double-decker London buses.

In 1988, the agency took over the Queensway ice-skating facilities. It was obviously before health and safety got its choke grip on fun, as people skated, skidded, staggered and careered around, sipping champagne from real glasses. The party in 1989 is reckoned by many to be the peak. Charlotte Street was recreated in Alexandra Palace. The food and style of numerous Charlotte Street restaurants was duplicated. So too was the agency's local pub, The Carpenter's Arms. Double-decker buses, street signs, parking meters, street cleaners, and a British Telecom workman's hut were all dressed into the lavish 'set'. Again, thousands of bottles of Lanson Black Label champagne (a client at the time) were drunk.

Lyn organized summer parties too, in the agency car park, which was cleared of cars and carpeted for the occasion. A beach party one year featured real camels. When they were being loaded back onto trucks after their work of giving rides to Saatchi people was done, one managed to escape, startling motorists in a number of nearby streets as it went on an unscheduled, liberated tour of the area. Saatchi & Saatchi have also held their own World Cup and Olympics at London's Crystal Palace. Any benefit derived from these healthy pursuits was promptly reversed, in all likelihood, during the huge marquee parties that followed these events.

The agency even held a major party to celebrate *losing* McDonalds, as Marilyn Baxter recalls. Maggie Taylor (who went on to be one third of the breakaway agency, Cowan Kemsley Taylor) adds, 'the agency parties were legendary but account group lunches weren't bad either. One I remember was a boating expedition with a picnic, accompanied, for some reason, by a number of Ann Summers sex-shop purchases…And then there was the private helicopter, commissioned from Battersea Heliport, to take us to lunch on the Isle of Wight…'

A couple of other individual demonstrations of passion, but almost devoid of physical violence, should be recorded. 'Paul Arden arrives to find his car space (which used to be Charles's, so it really matters to Paul) has Bill Muirhead's car in it', Paul Bainsfair explains. 'So he heads for Muirhead's office to find the door shut. Muirhead's secretary says, "You can't go in there. He's got the marketing director of BA with him." Apoplectic with rage, Arden storms in anyway and marches up to Muirhead. He's suddenly lost for words. At which point, he stubs out his big cigar in the plate of sandwiches they're sharing, turns on his heels and leaves. "Who's that?" asks the man from British Airways. "Fuck knows," says Muirhead.'

Bainsfair also recounts a prickly, clear-the-air client meeting with the Motor Cycle Association. The relationship wasn't good between account director Pete Watkins and the Association's director general. 'I knew Pete was combustible and pissed off with his client, so on the way to the meeting I stressed the need for a calm, considered and well-mannered meeting. "Don't worry," said Watkins, "I'll be as good as gold."

Smoked ham sandwich,
by Paul Arden.

'The meeting began with their president asking his DG to table one or two examples of where things had not been going smoothly. "Well," he began, "as I've told Pete on numerous occasions—"

He was interrupted by Watkins' first words of the meeting: "You fucking liar!"'

One can get a very clear sense of 'family' when evidence that great care extended from the product to the people is revealed. Charles and Maurice also led the way when it came to kindness and being compassionate and generous. Their sense of family was very well developed. When David Welch's father died, his request was for family flowers only, and contributions to a cancer charity. 'While we were viewing the family flowers, four pallbearers appeared, carrying an enormous floral tribute from Maurice and Charles. They also made the most generous contribution to the charity.'

On another occasion, Charles was trying to sell a white Mini he had. John Honsinger says he happened to mention, in a brief conversation, that he needed to get a car. 'Quick as a flash, Charlie told me to borrow the Mini for the weekend. First thing on Monday,

he was down my throat asking if I wanted to buy it. Hesitantly, I told him I loved the car, had enjoyed driving it, but I couldn't afford to buy it.' Without hesitation, because Honsinger said he liked it, Charles just gave him the car. 'No one had ever been so generous, and for me, this single gesture speaks volumes about the man behind the mask.'

Copywriter David Bourne tells another tale of great, unexpected generosity: 'I was leaving Saatchis, leaving London, leaving – if you shared Charles's anti-Antipodean view – civilization itself, to move with my Kiwi wife and wee baby daughter to Sydney and work for another agency. "So how are you getting there?" asked Charles.

"The agency is flying us out, business class. Why?"

"Simon!" Charles called out to his PA. "Get David's tickets changed to first class."'

Inspired by Maurice's speech she'd heard at a big Saatchi conference over a weekend on the south coast about 'nothing is impossible', account executive Jo Sacks thought she'd test it. On the Monday, she wrote to Maurice saying she was getting married and, if nothing was impossible, how would he feel about lending her one of his vintage cars for the wedding? 'I sat in trepidation for a few hours wondering if I'd overstepped the mark. Then there was a phone call from his PA. "About your letter to Maurice, Jo," he said, not sounding happy. "He says, which one would you prefer: a 1964 Bentley, or a 1963 Rolls? And he'll throw in Mick the Merc [his regular driver] as well." We took the Bentley.'

In a moment of pure compassion, Paul Arden tore up one of his creative's redundancy letters during the actual redundancy meeting because, according to Kate Morris, then head of HR, 'The creative told him his wife was expecting twins.'

Director of strategic planning in London and later CEO in Sydney, David Stewart-Hunter tells a particularly moving story: 'Charles and Maurice earned my undying commitment after my three-month-old daughter died, a cot death.

'Many of my agency friends and colleagues wrote letters of condolence, but the first, the very first, came from Charles who wrote, on behalf of Maurice and himself, in a most feeling and sympathetic way…I have never forgotten that. I don't care if it sounds sentimental: in my experience, it typified the agency – if you were part of the family then you would be looked after.'

Account director Mike Tomlin picks up on David's observation. 'It never ceased to amaze me what a close-knit family we were. This camaraderie was emphasized when a close workmate and friend – and one of the star players in my Saatchi seven-a-side rugby team – [account supervisor] Tim Dicken died in a motorbike crash. I attended Tim's funeral, fully expecting no more than about twenty or thirty people to be there. I didn't count them, but there must have been well over a hundred people who turned up. This was evidenced again when I too was involved in a near-fatal car crash. The overwhelming generosity and support I got – whilst recovering in hospital and afterwards – was just astounding.'

Wit and fun played a big role in the culture of Saatchi & Saatchi and it was sometimes used to lighten serious episodes. Dave Wood recalls a card (his favourite) especially created for, 'My dear mate, Alan Midgley, art director extraordinaire and card-carrying

Yorkshireman.' Midgley had come off second best in a road rage incident. In fact he'd been knifed and was seriously injured. The get well card was a mock-up of the cover of *Campaign* magazine with the faked headline:

'MIDGLEY STABBED – 72 ACCOUNT EXECS HELD FOR QUESTIONING'.

'Better still,' Wood reports, 'inside, some wag had written: "Stabbed in the front? Couldn't be anyone from Saatchis."'

In the prevailing culture, even highly sackable offences tended to go unpunished. When the overriding attitude is 'naughty and fearless' as Sean O'Connor put it, perhaps the very low sacking rate isn't surprising. And anyway, many candidates for the boot had probably only committed what could be described as crimes of passion.

For example, Paul Arden was so unhappy with the way a commercial for Disprin had turned out, he effectively ran away with the master tape to prevent it appearing on TV. No one knew where he'd gone with the tape. Charlie Sampson, the newly promoted account director on the business, realized the seriousness of the situation – two million pounds' worth of airtime booked and, with just two days to go, no film. He turned to Bill Muirhead, the agency chairman at the time. 'I explained about Paul running off with the master tape. He managed to get Paul on the phone and as Bill spoke to him explaining why he had to return the tape, I could make out Paul's voice protesting, "but it's not fucking good enough".

'Bill was getting nowhere despite his legendary powers of persuasion. I waited to see what Bill's next move would be. He picked up the phone and dialled a number. "Charlie, it's Bill. Arden's only gone and done it again!" He explained the situation to Charles and finished with the question, "Can I fire him this time?" Only one man could persuade Paul to hand back the master: Charles Saatchi. And he did.'

Nick Crean, the Saatchi brothers' PA, recalls another sackable offence that passed without incident: 'One lunchtime, Maurice was at his desk and wanted an apple, and he phoned down to the kitchen himself. "Hello," he said, "do you by any chance have an apple?" The legendary housekeeper, Joan, succinctly replied, "We're not a fucking orchard!" and hung up! Gosh, was Maurice angry.'

Joan was stone-cold sober, but it's true to say that over-refreshment was not an unusual occurrence in the Saatchi & Saatchi workplace. Art director Dave Hillyard went 'for a long boozy lunch with a couple of other creatives, Keith Terry and Dave Fowle. We got back to the agency about five o'clock, absolutely lashed. Dave Fowle passed out in the lift. Keith and I grabbed one foot each and started to drag him down the long corridor towards his office. The executive creative director at that time, Simon Dicketts, emerged at the other end of the corridor, walking towards us. "That's it," I thought. "We've had it. Oh well, it's been fun working here." As Simon approached, a broad smile appeared on his face. "Pleasant lunch, gentlemen?" "Yes...er...thank you," I replied nervously. "Excellent. Excellent." At that moment, I knew this was the place for me'.

And what a place. 'Place' means more than a postal address here, of course. It means, above all, a culture. Saatchi & Saatchi's culture is extraordinarily family-like. Adam Crozier remembers that the break up, when the brothers left in 1995, was very emotional and that people felt personally abandoned. It was a culture that embraced fall-outs and fights, love and forgiveness. It thrived on candour and passion and care. Care for its product and care for its people. Perhaps Saatchis shied away from good manners because they might get in the way of clarity and purpose. It recognized that volatility and incompatible chemistries can produce amazing results simply by shaking out complacency and cosiness.

How creative can a business be if there are no sparks, no passionate disagreements and too much compromise and easy pragmatism? It subscribes to the rhetorical, 'How can you trust anyone who always agrees with you?'

Rules are inconveniences. Mediocrity is deadly.

What really counts are the attributes of fearlessness and nerve. Cheek and cunning. Audacity and verve. Chutzpah and chutzpah.

SAATCHI & SAATCHI TIMELINE

Year Milestone

1970 Brothers Charles (twenty-seven) and Maurice (twenty-four) Saatchi open Saatchi & Saatchi in Golden Square, London W1 with ad in *The Sunday Times* 'Why I think it's time for a new kind of advertising'.

1973 Saatchi & Saatchi starts acquisition spree buying Manchester agency E. G. Dawes. Move to larger premises at 15 Lower Regent Street.

1974 Agency doubles in size with the acquisition of Notley Advertising and George J. Smith.

1975 S&S reverse takeover of Stock Exchange listed Compton UK. Partners, Saatchi & Saatchi Garland-Compton becomes the UK's fourth largest ad agency, eventually becoming Saatchi & Saatchi plc. Move in together to Garland-Compton's Charlotte Street offices.

1978 S&S gets headline press with new style of aggressive political advertising for the opposition party, the Conservatives. 'Labour Isn't Working' poster becomes one of the most iconic ad images of all time.

1979 Through further takeovers Saatchi & Saatchi becomes the UK's biggest agency. Margaret Thatcher becomes first female UK prime minister.

1980s Creativity flourishes throughout the Saatchi & Saatchi network, wining top awards in major worldwide competitions for advertising creativity.

1982 Saatchi & Saatchi buys US-based Compton Communications network – 'the biggest takeover in the history of advertising' – and overnight becomes a top ten worldwide advertising network.

British Airways moves its account to the new worldwide network – without a pitch. 'Nothing is impossible' becomes S&S motto.

1986 Saatchi & Saatchi plc buys another major US agency, Dancer Fitzgerald Sample, founded in 1923. DFS was among the twenty largest worldwide agencies.

The acquisition of Ted Bates Worldwide for $450 million makes Saatchi & Saatchi the world's biggest advertising agency. Key ambition achieved.

Yet another major US agency, Backer & Spielvogel, is purchased, and a second worldwide network is created: Backer Spielvogel Bates Worldwide.

1987   Dancer Fitzgerald Sample merged with Saatchi & Saatchi Compton to create Saatchi & Saatchi Advertising Worldwide.

1991   Saatchi & Saatchi Advertising Worldwide becomes the second largest international network in the world and is named 'International Agency of the Year'.

The Saatchi & Saatchi New Directors' Showcase launched in Cannes.

1994   Acrimonious shareholder protests challenge Saatchi & Saatchi plc corporate practices.

1995   Maurice Saatchi removed as chairman of Saatchi & Saatchi plc, and Charles quits. They lose legal battle to retain company name. Saatchi & Saatchi plc changes its name to Cordiant plc.

M&C Saatchi launched in competition with Saatchi & Saatchi.

1996   Saatchi & Saatchi London wins Agency of the Year at Cannes.

1997   Kevin Roberts appointed CEO of Saatchi & Saatchi. S&S de-merges from Cordiant, drops 'advertising' from its name.

2000   Paris-based Publicis Groupe SA acquires Saatchi & Saatchi for US $1.5 billion.

2002   Saatchi & Saatchi wins more Cannes Lions than any other network ever. S&S London wins 'Agency of The Year', also at Cannes. Nominated 'Creative Network of the Year' by Ad Age and 'wins more pan-regional and global new business than any other network' in Ad Age.

2003   Saatchi & Saatchi awarded Global Agency Network of the Year by AdWeek.

2010   Saatchi & Saatchi celebrates its fortieth birthday by hosting a joint party with M&C Saatchi for past and present alumni at the Saatchi Gallery, and special guests include, amongst others, ex-prime ministers Margaret Thatcher and John Major.

PICTURE CREDITS

85   Delta Times Square poster; Ed Bailey/ AP/PA Images

87   Photo of BA chairman Lord King; Peter Jordan / Alamy

88   Ginger crab poster; compilation courtesy of Paul Burns

89   T-Mobile dance TV advertisement still; T-Mobile

93   First Over the Wall poster; courtesy of Saatchi & Saatchi

95   Photo of Lord Dobbs; photography by Anders Birger; courtesy of Dobbs/Birger

99   Photo of Charlotte Street front doorstep; courtesy of Saatchi & Saatchi

100   Photo of Paolo Ettorre and Federico Fellini; courtesy of Annette Ettorre

101   Photo of rival Serie A teams; courtesy of Annette Ettorre

102   Furry Friends TV ad still; courtesy Solid Fuel Association

104   Mud Men, Papua New Guinea; courtesy of Sebastião Salgado

105   British Airways World's Biggest Offer advertisement; British Airways

106   Concorde image; Ace Stock Limited / Alamy.

      Red flag image; Andy Ryan / Getty Images

106   Full moon image; Mark Bond / Dreamstime

108   Rhino image; gualtiero boffi / Shutterstock

110   Man with laptop by pool image; Christo / Shutterstock

117   Flipchart image; Kolesov Sergei / Shutterstock

120   Toyota MR in S&S reception; courtesy of Saatchi & Saatchi

121   Fancy socks illustration; Freddie Darke

124   Lucio Fontana's slashed canvas; B Christopher / Alamy

132   Photo of chauffer; Dean Drobot / Shutterstock

134   Full moon image; Marbo / Dreamstime

136   Lasagna image; Lapina Maria / Shutterstock

142   Parrot image; Eric Isselee / Shutterstock

143   Solidarity logo; courtesy of Jerzy Janiszewski

146   Hungarian office photo; courtesy of Imre Kovats

152   Swan image; blickwinkel / Alamy

154   Cows image; Claudia Naerdemann / Shutterstock

158   Aeroplane image; motive56 / Shutterstock

160   Seafood red plate image; Steve Brown Photography / Getty Images

161   Nelson image; Andrew Holt / Getty images

164   Whale image; Andrey Nekrasov / Alamy

172   Miniature schnauzer image; Charlie Bard / Shutterstock

177   Alan Burles' champagne shot; courtesy of Alan Burles

180   White Mini image; Richard Grange / Alamy

Photography and illustrations other than those listed above are by Nick Darke.

Special thanks to the History of Advertising Trust for the time they have spent sourcing a number of images for this book.

ABOUT THE AUTHORS

RICHARD MYERS joined Saatchi & Saatchi in 1975 and created advertising for many significant clients including Anchor Butter, Black & Decker, British Airways and Castlemaine XXXX. He is married with three children and two grandchildren.

SIMON GOODE spent nearly thirty years at Saatchi & Saatchi, starting as business development director and later becoming general manager of the Europe, Middle East and Africa network. Dividing their time between London and France, he and his wife have two children and two grandchildren.

NICK DARKE was one of Saatchi & Saatchi's earliest recruits. After his role as creative director at Saatchi-owned Siegel & Gale, he became creative director of Saatchi & Saatchi Design. Nick now lives in Gloucestershire and works independently as a designer. He has two children and one granddaughter.

ACKNOWLEDGEMENTS AND THANKS

We want to acknowledge and thank the many people who have made this book possible, starting with all the 'insiders' who engaged with this project so enthusiastically and submitted their stories.

In addition, we're extremely grateful to Toni Arden, Alan Burles, Peers Carter, Holly Conville, James Cotier, Freddie Darke, Jackie Douglas, Graham Fink, History of Advertising Trust (Alistair Moir and David Thomas), David Miln, PICS (Keith Hall and Paul Tobutt), Kevin Roberts, Matt Ryan, Jeremy Sinclair and Jill Woolfenden.

The authors also want to acknowledge and thank their wives and families for their help, support and, above all, their remarkable patience.

If you think you deserve to be included here and you haven't been, we can only apologize.

INDEX

nonchalant approach 120
replacing accounts after 1995 split 127
Saatchi brothers and British Airways 128–9
shoo-ins 123–6, 132
spontaneity under pressure 116–17
stubborn determination 126–7
theatre/stunts 117–18, 119–20
see also selling ideas
New Directors' Showcase, Saatchi & Saatchi
102–3, 168
New York office 62–3, 158, 174
New Zealand office 52–3, 56–7, 101–2,
139–40
New Zealand Telecom 89, 101–2
Nicholls, Tim 53–4, 120
Nigeria 166
Nissan 160
Nizar 14
Nolan, Paul 72
Norden, Denis 50–1
Northern Ireland 71–2
Northwest Airlines 15
NSPCC (National Society for the Prevention
of Cruelty to Children) 70

O
O'Brien, Anne 28
O'Connor, Sean 6, 170, 182
office illusions, company 14–18
Oliver, Quintin 72
opportunism 59–60

P
Pallant, John 86, 118
Palmer, David 59
Panasonic 89
Paris office 84
Parker-Bowles, Simon 61
Parker, Mike 90–1, 111, 143, 172, 173
parties, agency 19, 175–8
party political broadcasts (PPBs) 15, 70–1
Pater, Lawson 20
Paul Weiland Film Company 87
pay rises 42–3
Perring, David 43

Perriss, John 91, 92
Pitcher, Patrick 117
P&O 76–7
Poland office 143–4
political campaigns
Nigeria 166
Northern Ireland 71–2
South Africa 71
see also Conservative Party
'pop-up' annual reports 93
Porsche 116
Pregnant Man campaign 68
press coverage, agency
national 9, 26, 66–7
trade 5–8, 23, 85, 91–2, 129
Primesite poster contractor 93
Procter & Gamble 47–8, 142, 143, 149,
153, 156, 157, 162, 174–5
Project Juno 112–14
public service announcements 68–70

R
radio 54, 58
RCA/Hitachi joint venture 160–2
Real Madrid FC 126–7
recruitment 26
dangerous/unlikely hires 32–4, 36–8
exceptional perks 31
expansion through acquisitions 36
graduates 38–41
imaginative job-seeking 29–32
interviews 26–9, 30, 43
publicity hires 35
staff retention 41–3
Rimmer, Ron 21–2
Ripa di Meana, Marquise Marina 70
Roberson, Sid 20
Roberts, Darby 32–3
Roberts, Kevin 61, 93, 126–7, 162–3
Rork, Andy 54
Roscow, Bob 160–2
Rover SD1 campaign 20–1
Ruane, Eugene 52–3
Rudaizky, John 126–7
Russell-Hills, Mike 15